Everything You Need to Know About

GEOGRAPHY
HOMEWORK

ANNE ZEMAN

KATE KELLY

AN IRVING PLACE PRESS BOOK

SCHOLASTIC INC.
NEW YORK TORONTO LONDON AUCKLAND
SYDNEY MEXICO CITY NEW DELHI HONG KONG

ISBN 978-0-545-37472-9

12 11 10 9 8 7 6 5 4 3 2 1   11 12 13 14 15 16/0

Printed in the U.S.A.   08

This edition first printing, September 2011

Cover design, Red Herring Design; Cover illustration, Sarajo Frieden
Interior design, Bennett Gewirtz, Gewirtz Graphics, Inc.; Interior illustration, Greg Paprocki

Grateful acknowledgment is made to:
NASA for permission to reprint photograph on page 9.

Contents

Part 4. Plants and Animals

Part 5. People on Land and Water

Appendix

Index

Introduction

It's time to do your homework—but you have questions. You need some help, but no adults are around, and you can't reach your classmates on the phone. Where can you go for help?

What Questions Does This Book Answer?

In *Everything You Need to Know About Geography Homework*, you will find a wealth of information, including answers to some of the most commonly asked geography homework questions, like

- Why do particular regions have different climates and what kinds of climates are there? The world's climate regions, or biomes, are described on pages 51–56.

- How do clouds affect climate? The effect of clouds on climate is explained on page 49.

- Why do we have seasons? Seasons are described on page 14.

- Where can I find descriptions of the U.S. states, including nicknames, state name origins, populations, and capital cities? "The U.S. in Focus," found on page 121, provides this type of information and more.

- How can latitude and longitude be used to locate major cities and other features on Earth? An explanation on how to use the geographic grid, which is formed by lines of latitude and longitude, is found on page 12.

- What are the different parts on a standard map? The parts of a standard map, including scale, compass, index, legends, and dates, are illustrated and defined on pages 26–29.

- What are the longest rivers in the world? The longest rivers in the world are listed and located on a map on pages 40–41.

- What are the names of the layers of the earth? A diagram describing the layers of the earth is found on page 30.

- Where are the border countries of the United States? All of the countries of the world and the states of the United States are shown on the maps illustrated in the Atlas, beginning on page 99.

- What are continents? How many are there? What are they called? Continents are defined and identified on page 31.

What is the *Everything You Need to Know About…Homework* series?

The *Everything You Need to Know About…Homework* series is a set of unique reference resources written especially to answer the homework questions of fourth-, fifth-, and sixth-graders. The series provides information to answer commonly asked homework questions in a variety of subjects. Here you'll find facts, charts, definitions, and explanations, complete with examples and illustrations that will supplement schoolwork colorfully, clearly, and comprehensively.

A Note to Parents

It's important to support your children's efforts to do homework. Welcome their questions and see that they have access to a well-lighted desk or table, pencils, paper, and any other books or equipment that they need—such as rulers, calculators, reference books or textbooks, and so on. You might also set aside a special time each day for doing homework, a time when you're available to answer questions that may arise. But don't do your child's homework for them. Remember, homework should create a bond between school and home. It is meant to enhance the lessons taught at school on a daily basis, and to promote good work and study habits. Although it is gratifying to have your children present flawless homework papers, the flawlessness should be a result of your children's explorations and efforts—not your own.

The *Everything You Need to Know About…Homework* series is designed to help your children complete their homework on their own to the best of their abilities. If they're stuck, you can use these books with them to help find answers to troubling homework problems. And remember, when the work is done, praise your children for a job well done.

Chapter 1 — Geography Defined

What Is Geography?

Geography is the study of the world, how it works, and how people use and change the world as they live in it. The word **geography** comes from the Greek words **geo**, meaning "earth," and **graph**, meaning "writing."

GEOGRAPHY EXPLORES MANY IMPORTANT QUESTIONS ABOUT WHERE AND HOW WE LIVE, INCLUDING:

1 What is the earth like?

2 Where are things located on the earth?

3 Who lives where on the earth?

4 Why is one place different from another?

5 How do people and places influence one another?

> A *geographer* is a person who studies geography. A professional geographer is a person who studies or teaches geography for a living or who uses geography in his or her job. For example, people who make road atlases or people who decide where new toy stores should be built may be geographers.

The Five Themes of Geography

Geographical thinking centers around five basic ideas, or themes.

1 PLACE

When a geographer says "place," he or she is talking about physical and human characteristics. Physical characteristics are the shapes of landforms and bodies of water, climate, soil, and plant and animal life. Human characteristics include the number of people living in a certain place, how close together they live, social traits, cultural traditions, and political institutions.

2 LOCATION

When a geographer says "location," he or she is talking about the importance of where one thing is in relation to another. When you study location, you study how physical characteristics (such as harbors, rivers, fertile plains, and mountainous terrain) affect human settlement and the ways in which places are used.

3 HUMAN AND ENVIRONMENTAL INTERACTION

When a geographer talks about human and environmental interaction, he or she is talking about the changes people have made in their environment and the changes they continue to make.

4 HUMAN MOVEMENT

A geographer who studies human movement follows the routes people take when they move from one place to another and tries to explain why these movements are necessary. He or she also studies the effects this movement has on the areas where people move and settle.

5 REGIONS

A geographer thinking about regions looks at what makes one area different from another. To do that, he or she studies physical and human characteristics to see where they change.

Social traits describe the things people do and say, and how they behave in groups. Social traits are influenced by population (see pp. 58–64) and culture (see pp. 65–74).

3

Geography and You

You don't need textbooks or classroom teaching to begin learning and using geography. In fact, you use geography every day—probably without realizing it.

MENTAL MAPS AND SKETCHES

Mental maps are maps you picture in your mind.

Close your eyes and imagine the inside of your bedroom. Where is the bed? How do you get from the bed to the bedroom door? Once you're at the door, which way do you go to get to the kitchen? How about from the kitchen to the front door? From your home to your school, playground, park, or grocery store?

If you are able to picture places in relation to one another, you are creating mental maps. Mental maps can be of any place, large or small. You will use mental maps all your life to help you understand where you are compared to other parts of your world.

A rough drawing of a mental map is a **map sketch**. If you draw your mental map on paper or on your computer, for example, you will have made a map sketch.

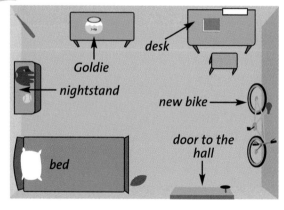

Our first mental maps are usually of our homes.

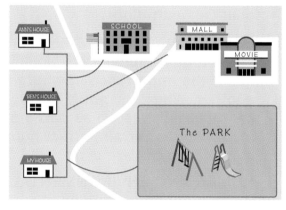

As we grow older, we create new maps to include neighborhoods and parks.

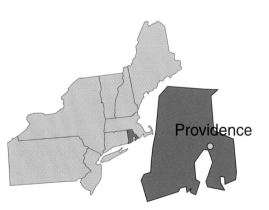

With more knowledge of the world, we are able to locate ourselves in larger areas. For example, we can think of our town within our state, our state within our country, our country within the world.

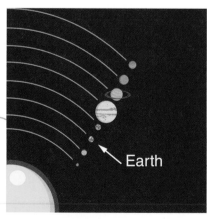

With still more knowledge, we can picture the earth in the solar system, the solar system in the galaxy, and the galaxy in the universe.

The Geography of Geography

Geography is about the "where" of things, so it's an important part of many subjects, including biology, weather sciences, history, and geology. Today, geographers usually study the geography important to one branch of learning. Among the many subfields of geography are:

1. **Agricultural geography**, the study of farming in different parts of the world.

2. **Biogeography**, the study of plants and animals in different geographic locations and climates.

3. **Cartography**, the science of making maps.

4. **Climatology**, the study of world climates.

5. **Cultural geography**, the study of people and their ways of life in different parts of the world.

6. **Geomorphology**, the study and measurement of landforms on the earth's surface and under water.

7. **Historical geography**, the study of how geography affected historical events.

8. **Industrial and marketing geography**, the study of locations for businesses and factories and how particular locations can benefit or hurt them.

9. **Meteorology**, the study of daily weather, including air temperature, precipitation (rainfall, snowfall, etc.), and winds.

10. **Political geography**, the study of nations and states, including the natural habitats, cities, farms, and populations within them.

11. **Resource geography**, the study of the location of natural resources and the conservation of those resources to meet human needs.

12. **Urban geography**, the study of how cities develop and work.

Galactic Address

A good first step toward making a mental map of yourself within the universe is to write your galactic address.

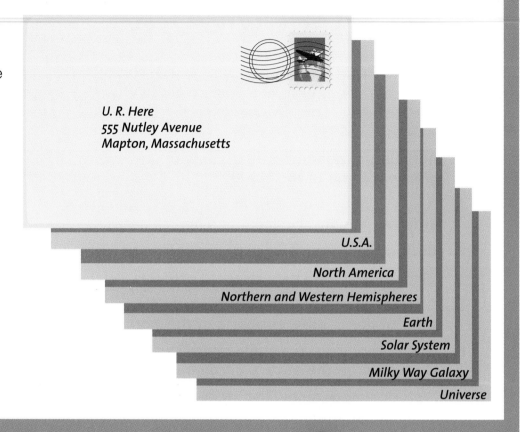

U. R. Here
555 Nutley Avenue
Mapton, Massachusetts

U.S.A.

North America

Northern and Western Hemispheres

Earth

Solar System

Milky Way Galaxy

Universe

Geographical Thinking

Picture yourself in Antarctica. What do you see? What are you wearing?
 Now picture yourself near the equator. Now what do you see? Are you wearing a parka and snow pants?

 You probably already know many geographical words and phrases that produce clear mental pictures. When you think of the word "cold," for example, do you think of "north," "south," "east," or "west"? If you live in North America, which direction makes you think of "hot"? What do you picture when you think "mountain," "valley," "city," or "swamp"?

 Geographical thinking is the ability to think about places and their characteristics. If Antarctica makes you think of a cold place or the equator of a hot one, you are thinking geographically.

Geographical thinking helps you select the appropriate clothes for climate and weather conditions, among other things.

The First Geographers

The first geographers were people who, like you, made mental maps and thought about things geographically. However, they didn't stop there. They traveled around, remembered what they saw, and recorded their experiences so other people could learn from them.

Early humans who followed animal migrations in order to hunt for food might be considered the first geographers. So, too, might those people who left their homelands to explore unknown areas and, later, returned to tell of their discoveries.

Thales: The First True Geographer?

Thales (c. 624–545 B.C.) was a man who lived on the shores of the Aegean Sea in Greece more than 2,500 years ago. He established methods for observing places. Thales traveled widely. He journeyed to markets far from his home to trade goods. Along the way, he wrote down all the new things he saw and learned. He also described a way to measure the distances and directions that set one place apart from another. His method was much like the systems of miles and kilometers we use to measure distances today. His information helped later geographers make accurate globes and maps (see p. 12). Because Thales was so careful about his observations, many scholars consider him one of the first true geographers.

The ancient Greeks were the first people to make a specific list of things to observe about places, such as the distance from other places or landmarks, the number of people in the place, the number of buildings, the sources of water, etc. Because of their attention to detail and careful descriptions, they are considered the first real geographers. The Greeks were also the first people to develop the theory that Earth is round, a theory proved to be true hundreds of years later.

Globes

Looking at Earth

A map of the solar system shows Earth in relation to the Sun and the other planets.

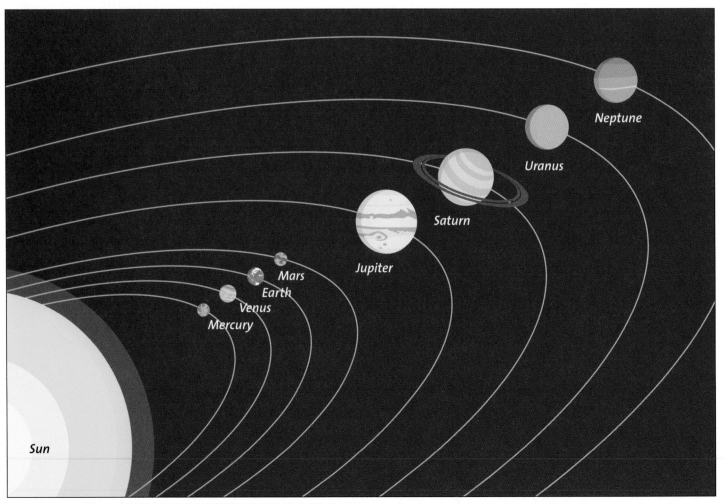

The solar system

This photograph of the earth from outer space shows water and land formations, as well as cloud cover.

Like the other planets, Earth is shaped like a sphere. From outer space, it looks like a disk covered by clouds.

But a photograph can show only half the earth—or one **hemisphere** (see p. 10). To show the whole earth, we use a *globe*, or a sphere-shaped model of the earth. Although it doesn't show all the cloud formations and wind patterns in the atmosphere, it does show the land and water formations on the earth's surface. Globes also help us understand natural events, among them day and night and the seasons.

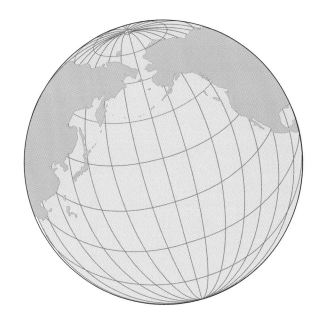
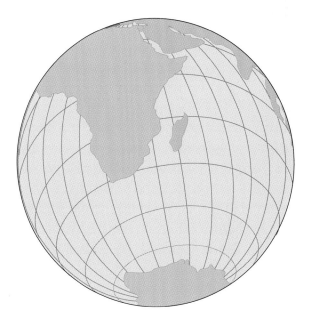

Globes show the water and land formations on the earth's surface.

Inventing the Globe

You can tell by photographs taken from space that the earth is round. But, if you look out a window at school or home, the surface of the earth appears mainly flat.

Yet more than 2,000 years before photography from space was possible, the ancient Greek geographers relied on observation and mathematics to figure out the shape and size of the earth. They made the first globes to show what the earth is shaped like.

Lines of Longitude and Latitude

The ancient Greeks also used their globes to think about the location of places on the earth. They divided the globe into 360 segments, called **degrees**. They used vertical **lines of longitude** to mark off the 360 parts. Longitude lines, also called **meridians**, are still used today to locate places on the earth, and to measure the distances between places. They can be seen on most globes.

The **prime meridian**, or 0 degrees (0°) longitude, was agreed upon in 1884. It passes through the site of the Royal Naval Observatory in Greenwich, England. Distance is measured east and west of this line. Longitude lines east of the prime meridian are numbered 1° through 179°. This is the **eastern hemisphere**. Longitude lines west of the prime meridian are also numbered 1° through 179°. This is the **western hemisphere**. The 180° line, reached by traveling east or west from the prime meridian, is exactly halfway around the earth from the prime meridian. Much of this line of longitude is also used as the **international date line** (see p. 15).

The ancient Greeks also drew lines to divide the earth horizontally. These lines are called **lines of latitude** or **parallels**. Latitude is measured from the **equator**, or 0 degrees (0°) latitude. Latitude lines are numbered from 0° to 90° from the equator to the north pole. The part of the earth from the equator to the north pole is called the **northern hemisphere**. Latitude lines are also numbered 0° to 90° from the equator to the south pole. The part of the earth from the equator to the south pole is called the **southern hemisphere**.

The northern hemisphere is divided into the tropics and the temperate zone at the Tropic of Cancer, a line of latitude that runs parallel to the equator at 23°30 north latitude. The temperate zone runs from 23°30 to the Arctic Circle, a line of latitude located at 66°30 north latitude. In the southern hemisphere, the Tropic of Capricorn, located at 23°30 south latitude, divides the tropics from the southern temperate zone. The temperate zone ends at the Antarctic Circle, or 66°30 south latitude.

Lines of latitude run parallel to each other; that means they never meet.

Degrees of longitude and latitude are divided into measures called *minutes*, and marked by the symbol ´. Like minutes in an hour, there are 60 minutes (60´) in a degree of longitude or latitude. Minutes are divided into seconds, and marked by the symbol ´´. There are 60 seconds in each minute of latitude or longitude.

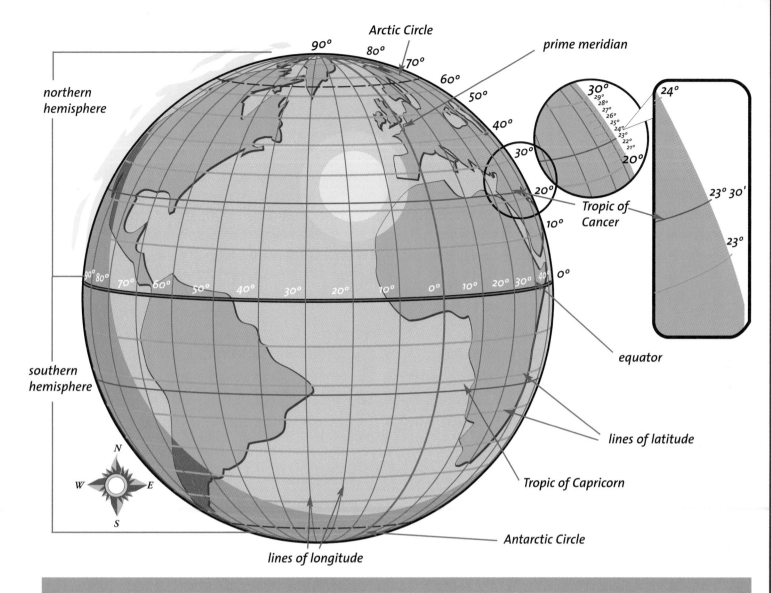

northern hemisphere

90° 80° 70° 60° 50° 40°

Arctic Circle

prime meridian

30°
29°
28°
27°
26°
25°
24°
23°
22°
21°
20°

24°

23° 30'

23°

Tropic of Cancer

10°

equator

southern hemisphere

lines of latitude

Tropic of Capricorn

Antarctic Circle

lines of longitude

The Two North Poles

The spot where the lines of longitude meet at the northernmost point of the globe is called the **north pole**. It is also called **true north**, or **geographic north**.

There is another north pole, called **magnetic north**. The magnetic north pole is not located in quite the same place as the geographical north pole, although they are very close. The difference between the location of the true north and magnetic north poles is shown on most globes.

You can find the magnetic north pole with a compass. A compass is made of a magnetized needle held up so that it turns freely. Because the earth itself is a huge magnet, no matter what direction you're going, the compass needle always points to magnetic north.

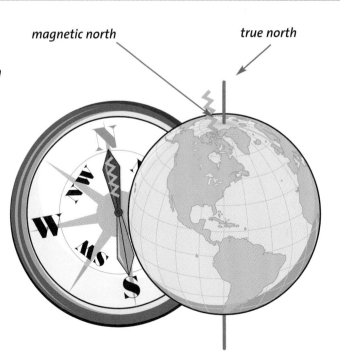

magnetic north

true north

Geographers in Ancient Greece

Greek geographers established the science of making highly accurate globes. The globes are based on some of the most important discoveries made by early Greek geographers.

Eratosthenes of Cyrene (c. 280–200 B.C.) used math and his knowledge of round objects (spheres) to measure the circumference of the earth. His measurement was close to the measurement used by scientists today (24,902 miles; 40,075 kilometers).

Hipparchus (born c. 150 B.C.) refined measurements for **latitude** and developed measures for **longitude** (see p. 10). He was the first to divide the equator into 360 degrees. Hipparchus also divided the world as he knew it into climatic zones (see p. 50) and drew the first known map of the night sky.

Strabo (60 B.C.–A.D. 25) described his travels through Europe, North Africa, and western Asia in a work called **Geographia**. Written as 17 volumes, *Geographia* describes in detail the world as the Greeks of his time knew it.

Claudius Ptolemy (2nd century A.D.) wrote an eight-volume book, also called **Geographia**. In it, he described in terms of longitude and latitude (see p. 10) all the places in the world that were known to the Greeks of this time.

The Geographic Grid

Lines of latitude and longitude form a **geographic grid**.

The geographic grid makes it possible to identify points on the earth and record their exact locations north or south of the equator and east or west of the prime meridian.

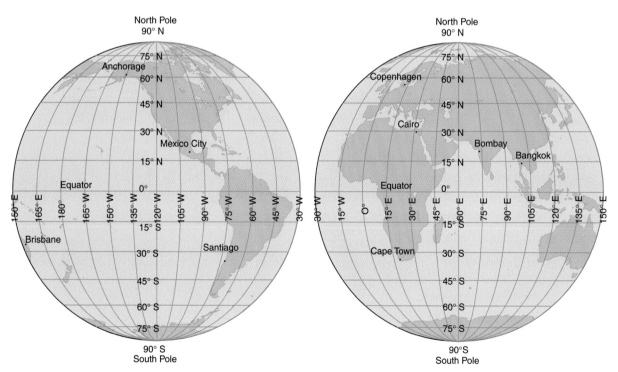

Using coordinates, or points of latitude and longitude, you can locate places on the earth's surface, including Anchorage, Alaska (61° north latitude, 150° west longitude), Bangkok, Thailand (14° north latitude, 100° east longitude), Bombay, India (19° north latitude, 73° east longitude), Brisbane, Australia (27° south latitude, 153° east longitude), Cairo, Egypt (30° north latitude, 31° east longitude), Cape Town, South Africa (34° south latitude, 18° east longitude), Copenhagen, Denmark, (56° north latitude, 12° east longitude), Mexico City, Mexico (19° north latitude, 99° west longitude), and Santiago, Chile (33° south latitude, 71° west longitude).

Light on Earth

Light on earth is a result of our planet's position in relation to the sun and moon. Our position in space results in such events as day and night, the seasons, solstices, eclipses, and tides.

DAY AND NIGHT

A globe and a lightbulb illustrate how day changes into night. Only half the surface of the globe is covered in light at any time.

As the globe rotates on its axis, the part of the surface that is lighted changes.

Just like the globe in the example, the earth rotates on an axis. As a particular place on the earth rotates out of the sunlight, night falls. As that place rotates back into the light, day dawns.

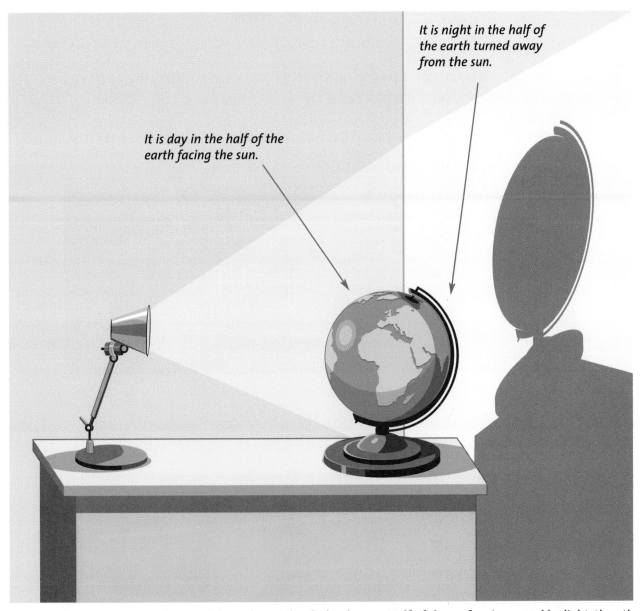

It is night in the half of the earth turned away from the sun.

It is day in the half of the earth facing the sun.

A lightbulb shining on a globe shows how the earth is lit by the sun. Half of the surface is covered by light, the other half is in shadow. As the earth rotates on its axis, every point on the earth moves from the light, or day, to shadow, night, and back again.

THE SEASONS

A globe and a lightbulb can also illustrate how the seasons change. Earth not only rotates on its axis, it also orbits the sun. The angle of the axis is tilted in relation to its orbit. When the earth is positioned so that the northern hemisphere is tipped toward the sun, it is summer there and winter in the southern hemisphere.

A lightbulb and four globes show how the earth is lit by the sun at various points in its orbit.

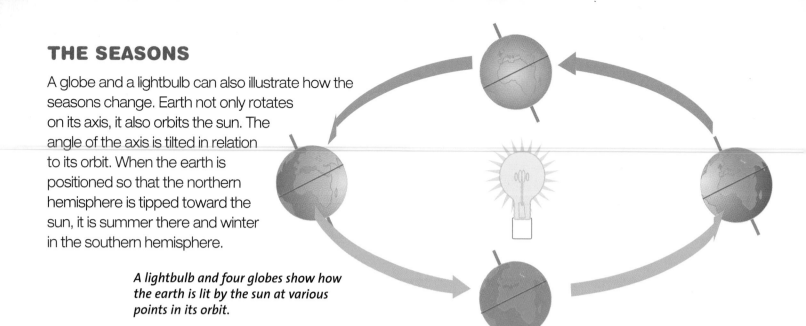

ECLIPSES

Occasionally the light from the sun or the sunlight reflected off the moon is kept from hitting the earth, or **eclipsed**, by the position of the earth and moon in relation to the sun.

A **solar eclipse** occurs when the moon passes between the earth and the sun. People standing in the shadow see the moon pass in front of the sun, blotting out its light.

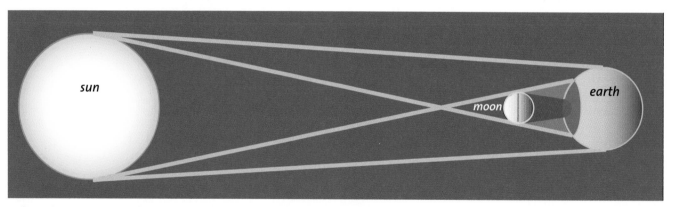

solar eclipse

A **lunar eclipse** occurs when the earth passes between the sun and the moon. People on the side of the earth facing the moon see the moon pass from sunlight into the shadow cast by the earth.

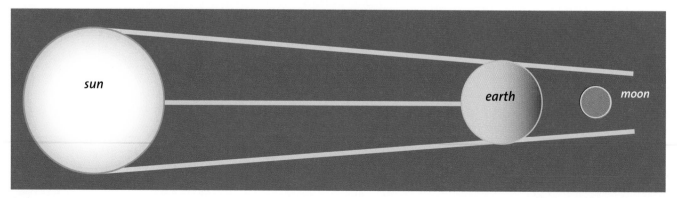

lunar eclipse

14

The 24-Hour Globe: Time Zones

In addition to lines of longitude and latitude, the globe is marked off into 24 **time zones**. The time zones run in the same direction as the lines of longitude, and begin at 0 degrees (0°), or the **prime meridian**. The time zone that lines up roughly along 180° longitude follows the **international date line**. Places to the east of this line are a calendar day behind places to the west. If you fly from west to east over the international date line on Saturday, you fly into Friday. You gain one day on your trip.

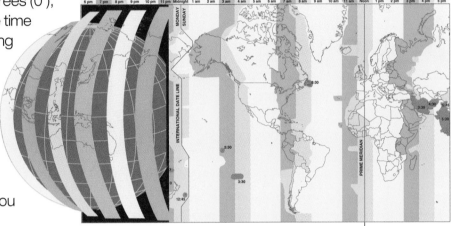

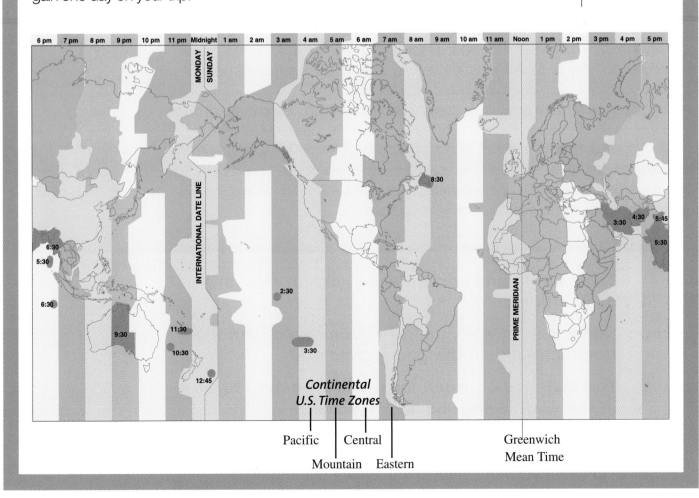

Continental U.S. Time Zones

Pacific   Central

Mountain   Eastern

Greenwich Mean Time

Chapter 2

Maps

What Is a Map?

A ***map*** is a picture of a place on a flat surface. Most maps show a place drawn from above.

Different types of maps show different types of information, such as natural features, where humans live, historical and modern political boundaries, centers of industry, and variations in climate and weather.

Map Projections

Imagine peeling the surface off a globe and laying it down flat. It would form a map with a very unusual shape.

Globes accurately show sizes, locations, and distances on the earth because the earth, like a globe, is roughly a sphere. Because they are flat, maps do not show the round earth exactly as it is shown on a globe.

In order to make maps, mapmakers use ***projections*** based on the geographical grid (see p. 12). In order to take the grid from a globe and open it flat on a map, the grid must be changed somewhat. These changes affect the accuracy of maps.

Standard map projections are created to represent the geographic grid as accurately as possible on flat surfaces. In inventing projections, mapmakers have four major concerns: area, direction, distance, and shape.

When mapmakers make projections, they must decide which elements need to be most accurate on their maps. If a map is going to be used to measure the distance between places, a mapmaker will choose a projection that shows the size of land and water areas as accurately as possible to scale. If a mapmaker needs to show direction and the shape of the land and water areas, he or she will choose a projection that depicts those features most accurately.

MAPMAKERS' CONCERNS

area	The size of land and water regions in relation to each other.
direction	North, south, east, and west compared with their true locations on the geographic grid.
distance	The distance between locations on a map relative to the earth's surface, called scale.
shape	The shapes of land and water areas compared with their shapes on the earth or a globe.

Some Common Map Projections

Conic
Used for mapping a large piece of the earth's surface, it shows accurate distance, direction, and shape for the limited area mapped.

Interrupted
(equal area)
Shows accurate area and shape. Oceans have open, pie-shaped interruptions to adjust for distance.

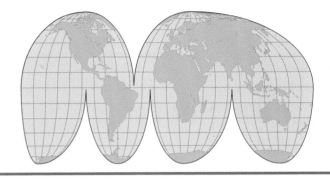

Mercator
(cylindrical)
Shows accurate direction, but land and water areas are greatly distorted toward the north and south poles.

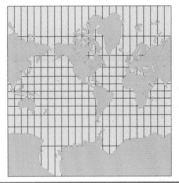

Polar
(azimuthal)
Used for mapping hemispheres instead of the whole earth; shows accurate distance and direction, but shape and size become more and more distorted toward the edges.

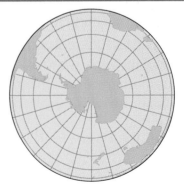

Robinson
(oval)
Shows accurately the shape and size of continents, but the water areas are expanded to fill the extra space.

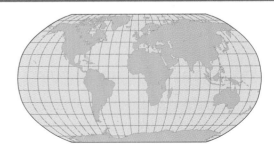

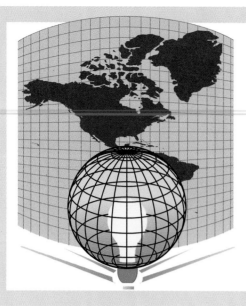

How Map Projections Are Made

Put a projector light inside a globe. The spaces formed by the geographic grid when **projected** from the globe onto a flat screen will change as the projector light is moved. While the location of a city is likely to fall in the same place on the globe and its projection, the sizes and shapes of countries and continents will change as the distances away from the center of the projected image change. Areas on the edges of the map appear stretched as they are flattened in the projection.

When cartographers make maps, they use mathematical calculations to project the geographic grid (see p. 12) onto paper.

Natural Features

Natural features are features on the earth's surface that were not made by humans. These features include nonliving things (rocks, minerals, soil, water, and atmosphere) as well as living things (plants and animals).

PHYSICAL FEATURES

Earth's nonliving, or **physical**, features include mountains, plains, rivers, lakes, and oceans. The earth's physical features are constantly changing. A number of forces, such as erosion and weathering, gradually wear down the earth's surface. Other forces, such as fire, earthquakes, and volcanoes, make almost instant changes (see pp. 32–33).

ATMOSPHERIC FEATURES

The earth's nonliving features also include **atmospheric** conditions, or climate and weather. Climate is the usual weather in a place over a long time period. It, along with physical features, determines which plants and animals can live in a particular place (see pp. 43–49).

LIVING FEATURES

Earth's living features are its plants and animals, including humans. Different plants and animals thrive in different natural regions, or **biomes** (see pp. 50–56). Biomes are large environments that share the same general temperature and annual rainfall.

> **Cartography** is the art of making maps or charts. People who draw maps are called **cartographers**. The words come from the Latin **carta**, meaning "map," and the Greek **graph**, meaning "writing."

Human-made Features

Human-made features are features on the earth's surface created by human beings—for example, buildings, monuments, parks, roads, fields, and landfills.

The First Maps

No one knows for certain who made the first maps or what those maps looked like. But we know that humans have been making maps for thousands of years. Scratched into sand, painted on animal skins, carved into wood, or drawn on rock walls, maps helped people avoid danger, find good hunting grounds, and locate clean water. The ancient Egyptians even supplied maps to tax collectors to help them along their routes.

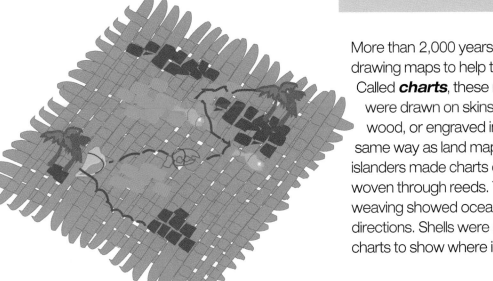

More than 2,000 years ago, Europeans were drawing maps to help them navigate at sea. Called **charts**, these maps of waterways were drawn on skins and stones, carved in wood, or engraved into clay—in much the same way as land maps were made. Pacific islanders made charts out of palm leaves woven through reeds. The pattern of the weaving showed ocean currents and wave directions. Shells were attached to the reed charts to show where islands were located.

The oldest maps that exist today were made in the ancient Middle Eastern civilization of Babylon. These maps are more than 4,000 years old, and are etched into large clay tablets.

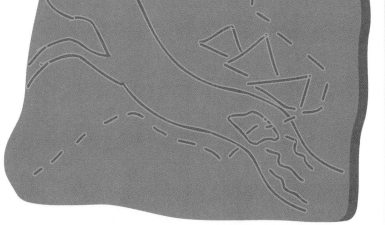

Three Basic Kinds of Maps

Geopolitical maps show political and physical features on one map. (See p. 28 for an example of a geopolitical map.)

POLITICAL MAPS

Political maps show how humans have divided up the earth's surface. They show borders between countries, the locations of cities and towns, building sites, neighborhoods, settlement plans, roadways, and other human-made features.

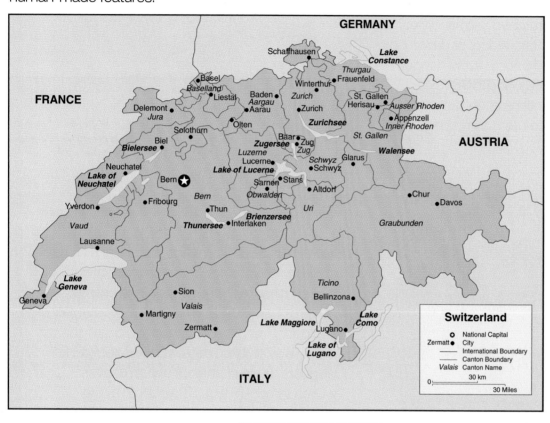

This political map of Switzerland shows the countries it borders, as well as its cantons (states) and major cities.

PHYSICAL MAPS

Physical maps show the land formations and water on the earth's surface. Physical maps show mountains, valleys, plains, oceans, rivers, and lakes. They can also show locations of natural plant life, water currents, and wind patterns.

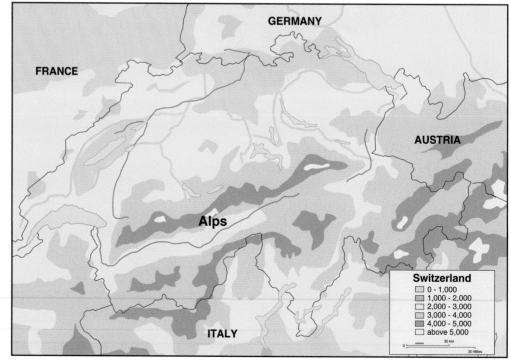

This physical map of Switzerland shows variations in the elevation of the land, as well as the locations of major rivers.

CULTURAL MAPS

Cultural maps show such patterns as ethnic groups, religious practices, languages spoken, customs, educational levels, and recreational choices.

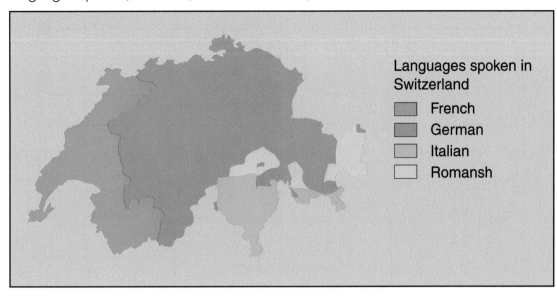

This cultural map of Switzerland shows where different languages are spoken within the country.

Charts

Charts are maps of bodies of water. Sailors use them to navigate in open ocean waters as well as on lakes and in shallow bays, inlets, and rivers. Charts show water depths, currents, and physical features found below the surface of the water. They also locate ports and places to anchor safely, as well as buoys, lighthouses, and other aids to seafarers.

The depth of water is shown in feet on this sample chart.

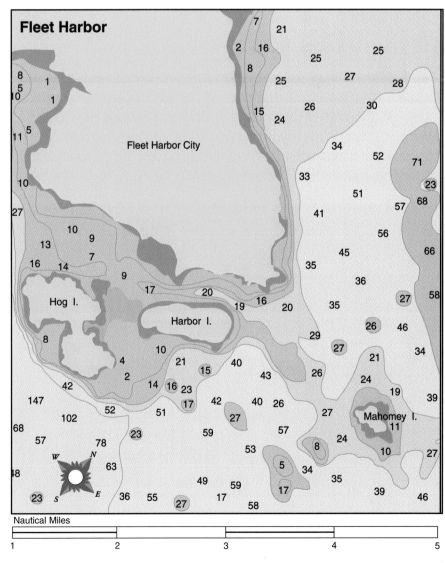

Maps for Special Uses

RELATIVE LOCATION MAPS

Relative location maps show the position of a place in relation to its surroundings. For example, such a map might show where a specific place is located in relation to the rest of the world.

In shopping malls, relative location maps show where you are standing in relation to the rest of the mall and its stores.

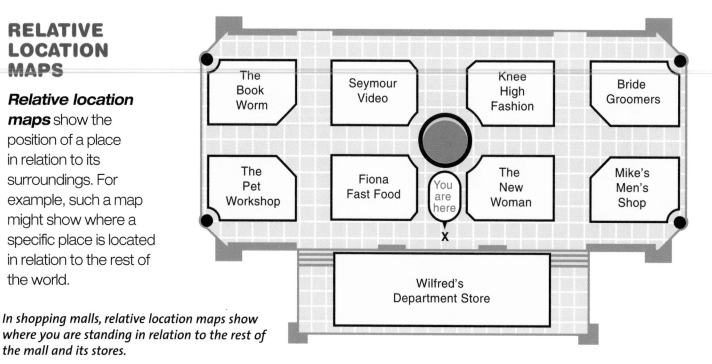

DISTRIBUTION MAPS

Distribution maps show how things are spread out across an area or throughout the world. For example, distribution maps may show where sheep are raised on all the continents or where oil wells are located in Oklahoma. Distribution maps can also show where rain forests and timber mills are located, what kinds of rocks make up the earth's surface, or where bookstores are located in your hometown.

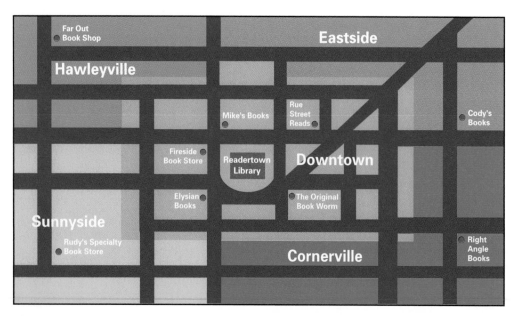

This distribution map shows the location of bookstores in Readertown. According to the map, most bookstores are downtown, and the rest of Readertown's bookstores are evenly distributed in the residential neighborhoods.

TOPOGRAPHIC MAPS

Topographic maps show physical features, and are often drawn showing **contours**, or lines that show differences in elevation. Any topographic map drawn to show contours may also be called a **contour map**.

This section of a topographic map shows color-keyed contours, as well as a variety of physical features: roads, railroad tracks, bridges, and an air strip.

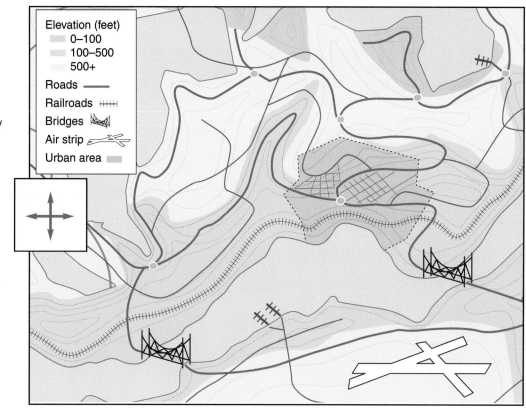

CLIMATE AND WEATHER MAPS

Climate and **weather maps** show how and where climatic and weather conditions occur across a region or throughout the world.

Weather map illustrating a fall day in the United States

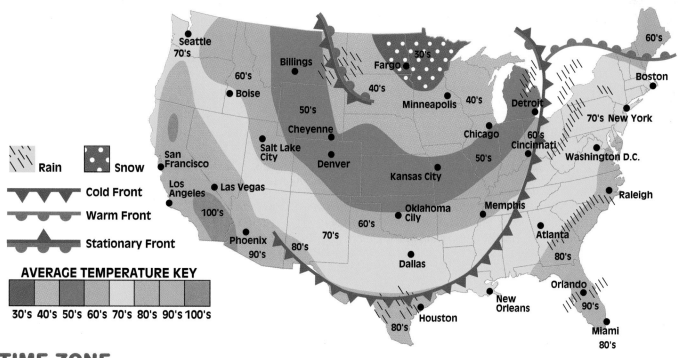

TIME ZONE MAPS

Time zone maps show how the earth is divided into different time zones.
(See p. 15 for an example of a time zone map.)

ALTERED STATES:
Cartograms

Cartograms are diagrams in map form. The places on a cartogram are drawn in mathematical proportion to show how much of a particular thing is found in each mapped area.

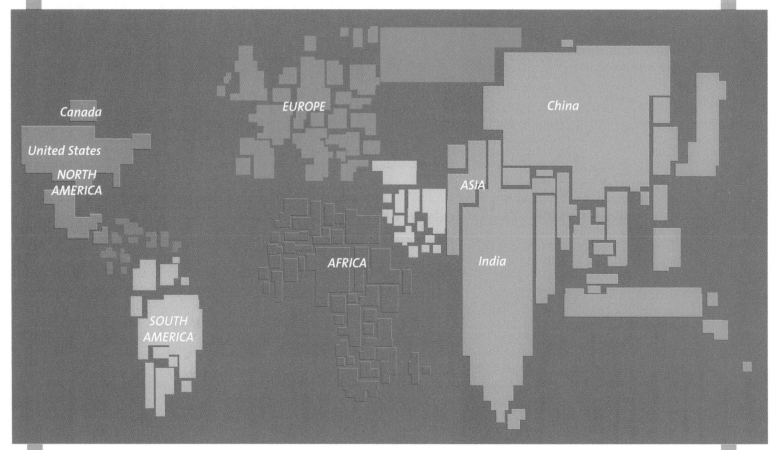

Drawn from data collected from the U.S. Bureau of the Census International Database

A cartogram of world population shows China and India as much larger than North American and European countries. Anyone looking at this cartogram can tell at a glance that there are more people in China than in the United States and Canada combined.

Written References:
Geographical Dictionaries and Almanacs

Maps and globes are the most important tools you will need to do your geography homework, but **geographical dictionaries** and **almanacs** are very useful, too.

Hoth·am, Mount \-'häth-əm\. Mountain in the Darg Plateau, E Victoria, SE Australia, SW of Mt. Kosciusko; 6108 ft.

Ho–t'ien \'hō-'tyen\ *also* Kho·tan \'kō-'tän\. 1 River, W Sinkiang Uighur, W China; joins the Yarkand to form Tarim river, but dry much of the year.
2 Town, China. See KHOTAN 2.

Hotin. See KHOTIN.

Hot Spring. County in Arkansas. See table at ARKANSAS.

Hot Springs. 1 County in Wyoming. See table at WYOMING.
2 City, ⊗ of Garland co., W cen. Arkansas, in Ouachita Mts. 47 m. WSW of Little Rock; pop. (1970c) 35,631; health and tourist resort noted for its 47 thermal springs. Settled 1807; made, with surrounding area, a U.S. Government reservation 1832, **Hot Springs National Park** 1921 (see UNITED STATES, *National Parks*).
3 City, New Mexico. See TRUTH OR CONSEQUENCES.
4 City, ⊗ of Fall River co., SW corner of South Dakota, in foothills of Black Hills 48 m. S of Rapid City; pop. (1970c) 4434; health resort; thermal and mineral springs; sandstone quarries; mica, feldspar, gold, silver mines.
5 Village, Bath co., W Virginia, 5 m. SW of Warm Springs; mineral springs; Japanese diplomats interned here 1942 at beginning of war with Japan; scene of United Nations Conference on Food and Agriculture 1943.

Hot Springs Peak. Mountain, Humboldt co., NW Nevada; 6450 ft.

Hot Sul·phur Springs \-'səl-fər-\. Town, ⊗ of Grand co., N Colorado; pop. (1970c) 220; hot sulfur springs.

Hotte, Massif de la. See SUD, MASSIF DU.

Hot·ten·tot Point \ˌhät-ᵊn-ˌtät-\. Cape on SW coast of South-West Africa, N of Lüderitz.

Hou·dain \ü-'daⁿ\. Commune, Pas-de-Calais dept., N France, near Béthune; pop. (1962c) 8869; coal; has church (12th and 16th cents.); destroyed in World War I and rebuilt.

Hou·dan \ü-'däⁿ\. Village, Yvelines dept., N France; pop. (1962c) 2358; has 15th–16th cent. church and keep of an early 12th cent. castle; noted for its poultry market, the Houdan breed of domestic fowl originating here.

Hou·deng–Goe·gnies \ü-däⁿ-gər-'nyē\. Commune, Hainaut prov., SW Belgium, on a tributary of the Haine, E of Mons; pop. (1969e) 8947; coal mines, smelting, woodworking, rope making, glassworks.

Houf·fa·lize \ü-fə-'lēz\. Village, Luxembourg prov., SE Belgium, 10 m. N of Bastogne; pop. (1969e) 1346; taken by Germans in ~ly phase ~le of the Bulge Dec. 1944;

Geographical dictionaries, or gazetteers, are made up of alphabetical lists of geographic names. General gazetteers list all kinds of geographical features—including countries, cities, counties, landforms, bodies of water, and more—each followed by a brief description. The description usually tells the size and location of a feature, as well as how to pronounce its name. Gazetteers often define the location of a place by latitude and longitude coordinates, or by the number of miles it is from a well-known location.

Almanacs, unlike geographical dictionaries, are not organized alphabetically. Instead, they have detailed indexes to help you locate geographic information.

New Jersey
(see States, U.S.)
Admission, area, capital......386,640
Agriculture.............160,161,162,163
Altitudes (high, low)...................385
Birth, death statistics.................939
Bridges...............................622-624
Budget...154
Chamber of Commerce..............640
Commerce at ports 674
Congressmen.................74,579,583
Courts, U.S. 596
Debt..154
Ethnic, racial distribution............640
Fair..640
Geographic center 387
Governors 598,601
Income, per capita 640
Interest, laws, rates....................713
Marriages, divorce laws722-723,942
Name, origin of..........................388
Population 129

Parts of a Map

Elevation *means the height of land above sea level. It is shown on maps using contour lines. Elevation can also be shown using shading or colors.*

The *directional arrow* *shows the directions—north, south, east, and west, and sometimes northwest, northeast, southeast, and southwest—in relation to the map. These directions show the orientation of the map. Most world maps show north on the top and south on the bottom, east to the right, and west to the left. Maps of smaller areas often use this standard orientation, too. Some directional arrows are plain and simple. Others are decorated.*

A *compass rose* *is an ornamental directional arrow often used on ship charts and old-fashioned maps. The rose is usually drawn from a circle divided into 360 degrees, and is used to tell directions from magnetic north, or 0 degrees (0°) on the compass.*

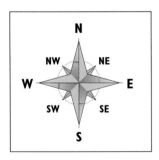

A *map index* *is included on some maps. It is a list of place names, complete with coordinates for finding the places on the map.*

Major Cities	
Bologna	D-2
Firenza	D-2
Genova	C-2
Milano	C-1
Palermo	E-4
Roma	E-3
Venezia	E-1

Symbols, *or* *icons,* *are used on maps to represent real objects or places. Symbols can be simple dots to indicate cities, pictographs (tiny pictures) to indicate products, or colors to show location. Symbols are explained in the map key or legend.*

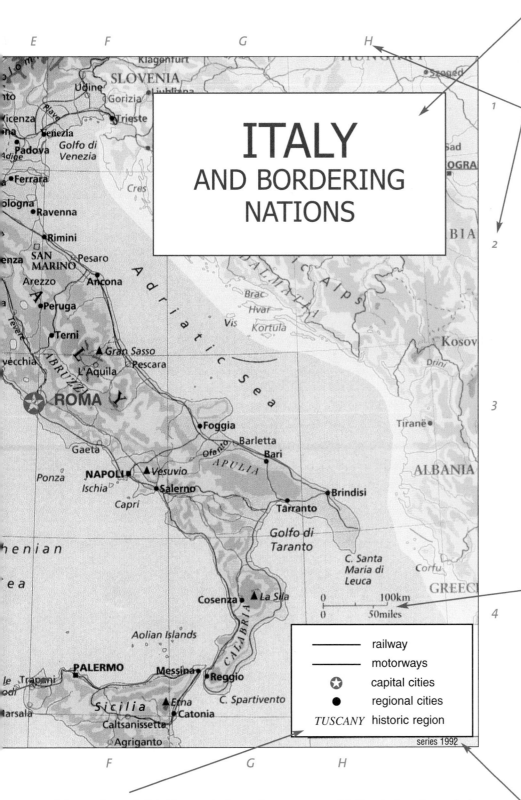

A *title* is included to tell map readers what the map is about.

Coordinates are a set of points or spaces, for example, G-2, located by using the map grid. The map index uses a map grid to help the reader find a specific location.

A *map grid* is a grid drawn on a map. You can read the map grid by looking in the margins of the map. The letters A, B, C, etc., run along the top and bottom margins. The numbers 1, 2, 3, etc., run along the left and right margins. If a place is identified at D-3, simply find the square on the grid where column D and row 3 intersect. The map grid may or may not follow the geographic grid of latitude and longitude. Many highway maps have their own grids.

The map *scale* shows how the size of the map relates to the size of a real place. It may be stated in words, in combinations of words and numbers, and in ratios. For example, if a map's scale is 1 inch=100 miles, one inch on the map represents one hundred miles in the real world.

A *key*, or *legend*, lists the symbols used on a map and tells what each symbol means. For example, on some maps, cities can be represented by different-sized dots. Large dots can stand for large cities and small dots for small cities or towns. Keys are usually set apart from the rest of a map, often in a box.

Dates appear on many maps to tell when the map was drawn.

27

Understanding and Comparing Maps

To understand a map, you must be able to "read" it.

Once you can read maps, you can compare maps. By comparing the information on different maps, you can learn how many features work together to make a place special. For example, if you compare a map of North American waterways to a map of North American cities, you'll find that most cities are located on waterways. This is important geographical information—it shows that water is one thing people think about when deciding where to live.

THREE STEPS TO READING MAPS

1 Look at the map *title*. It will tell you what type of information, as well as which region or location, is shown on the map.

2 Look at the map *scale*. Some maps are very simple. Others show a lot of detail. The amount and type of detail on a map depends on the map scale, or the size of the area shown on the map. For example, it would be difficult to show the location of houses on a map of your state. However, it would be a logical feature on a map of your neighborhood. Successfully reading a map means understanding its scale.

3 Look at the *legend*. The legend will tell you what the symbols on the map mean. In order to understand the map fully, you will need to understand the symbols and the type of information they convey.

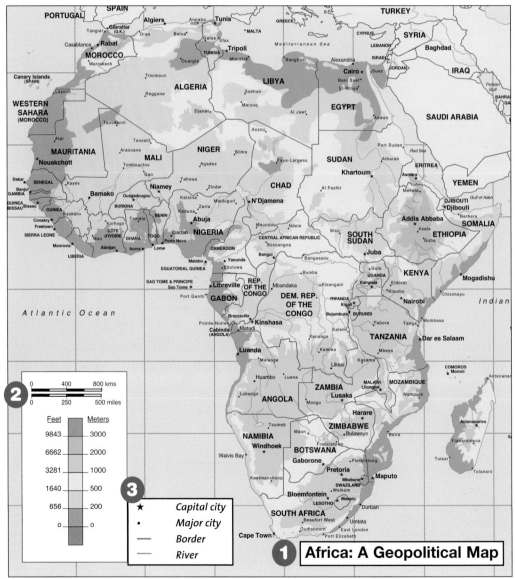

Africa: A Geopolitical Map

Three Steps to Comparing Maps

1 Choose maps that show information you want to compare.

2 Locate your area of interest on both maps.

3 Use the map symbols to read both maps. Then note how the maps are alike and how they are different. When you are using two or more maps, watch for map scale, the type of projections used (see p. 17), and the date the maps were published.

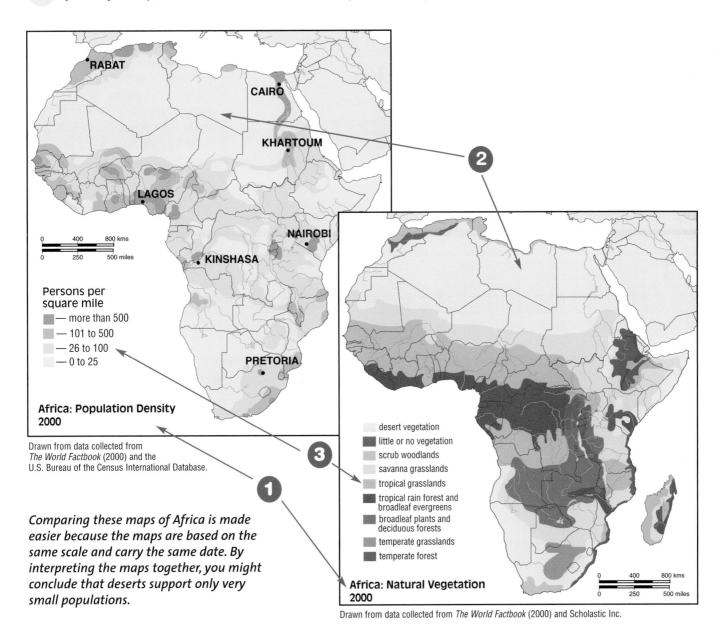

Africa: Population Density 2000

Persons per square mile
- more than 500
- 101 to 500
- 26 to 100
- 0 to 25

Drawn from data collected from *The World Factbook* (2000) and the U.S. Bureau of the Census International Database.

Comparing these maps of Africa is made easier because the maps are based on the same scale and carry the same date. By interpreting the maps together, you might conclude that deserts support only very small populations.

Africa: Natural Vegetation 2000

- desert vegetation
- little or no vegetation
- scrub woodlands
- savanna grasslands
- tropical grasslands
- tropical rain forest and broadleaf evergreens
- broadleaf plants and deciduous forests
- temperate grasslands
- temperate forest

Drawn from data collected from *The World Factbook* (2000) and Scholastic Inc.

Chapter 1 # The Land

How the Earth Was Formed

Geographers believe that about 4.6 billion years ago a cloud of dust particles came together to form a ball of melted rock. The ball cooled over several million years, forming the earth.

As the molten rock ball cooled, a thin solid layer formed over the surface of the earth. This layer is called the crust. The crust is about 2 miles thick under the deepest parts of the ocean and up to 75 miles thick under the tallest mountain peaks.

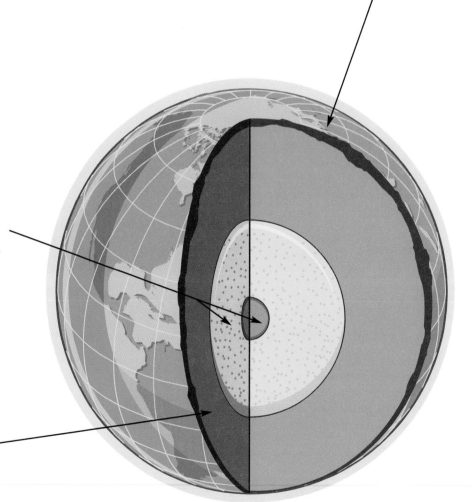

The earth's core has two parts: the outer core and the inner core. The outer core is made up of molten rock. The inner core is solid. The core has a radius of about 2,100 miles.

The mantle lies between the earth's crust and core. It is a layer of very hot, sometimes melted rock about 1,800 miles thick.

Plate Tectonics

Continents are the large landmasses on earth: Africa, Australia, Antarctica, North America, South America, and Eurasia. Eurasia is sometimes considered two continents, divided by the Ural Mountains and the Caspian Sea into Europe to the west and Asia to the east.

The crust of the earth is not one solid piece. It is broken into large pieces, called **tectonic plates**. The plates are like enormous ships that float upon the earth's mantle.

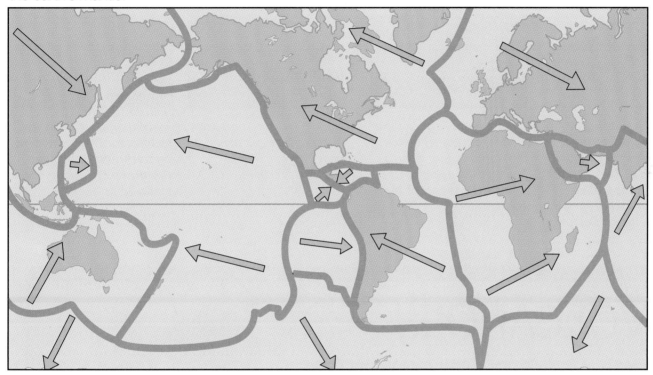

World map showing fault lines and the direction of tectonic plate movement.

FAULT LINES

Fault lines occur along the edges between tectonic plates. As the plates move, a number of tectonic events occur along the fault lines.

PANGAEA AND CONTINENTAL DRIFT

Scientists believe that about 200 million years ago, all the continents were connected. They formed a supercontinent that scientists call **Pangaea**.

Then the continents separated at places where the tectonic plates broke apart. Like ships on water, the plates slowly moved apart, and the continents we know today were formed.

The continents are still moving. This movement is called **continental drift**. In another 200 million years, the continents may be connected again or may drift into a completely different arrangement on the planet.

Tectonic Events That Shape the Land

Tectonic plates are moving in different directions at different speeds. The features on the surface of the earth tell us where the plates push beneath each other or collide.

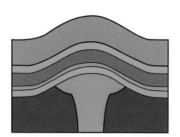

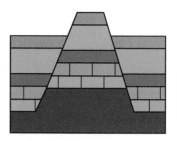

Most volcanoes form when molten rock from deep inside the earth rises to the surface at or near a fault line or a soft spot in a plate. The molten rock spurts out of the top of the volcano in the form of lava.

Dome mountains form when molten rock pushes up toward the earth's surface along a fault line but doesn't break through the surface of the earth.

Block mountains form when blocks of rock split along fault lines and slide in opposite directions.

Fold mountains form when tectonic plates move against each other and push and squeeze up the crust of the earth.

VOLCANOES

Volcanoes are mountains formed when the **magma**, or red-hot liquid rock and gases that lie below the surface of the earth, rises through vents and passages in the earth's surface and comes out as lava.

Not all volcanoes are **active**, or capable of erupting. In fact, scientists describe four types of volcanoes:

active	erupting constantly
intermittent	erupting at regular intervals
dormant	inactive, but expected to become active again
extinct	inactive for hundreds of years

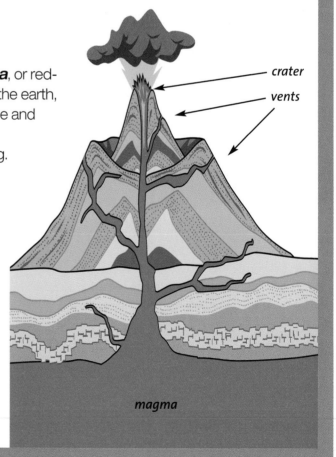

crater

vents

magma

EARTHQUAKES

Earthquakes are sudden shifting movements in the earth's surface. Some earthquakes cannot even be felt, yet others are strong enough to knock down skyscrapers and twist highways as if they were ribbons. Earthquakes happen when tectonic plates collide, separate, or scrape against one another along fault lines.

1

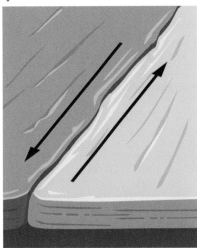

Forces push tectonic plates into one another, causing them to collide or scrape against each other.

2

Over thousands of years, the forces cause the rocks along the fault line to bend and twist.

3

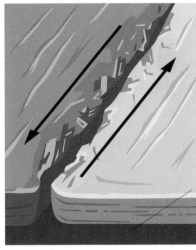

Finally, the force becomes so great that the rocks break loose and jolt past each other, causing an earthquake.

The Ring of Fire
Where Volcanoes and Earthquakes Often Happen

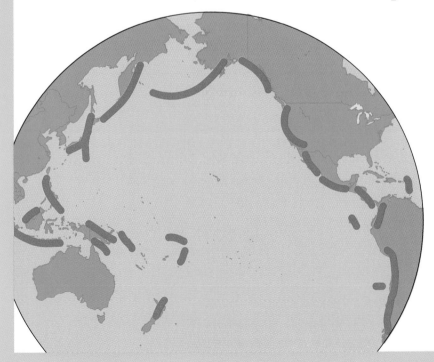

Volcanoes and earthquakes most frequently occur along the fault lines in the earth's tectonic plates. The "ring of fire" in the Pacific Ocean is the world's most active area of earthquake and volcanic activity. Why? The faults in the Atlantic are, for the most part, expanding, or moving away from each other. But in the Pacific, the plates are colliding, or rubbing up against each other (see above, also p. 31).

Landforms

Landforms are the natural features of the earth's land surface, including mountains, other highlands, plains, and lowlands.

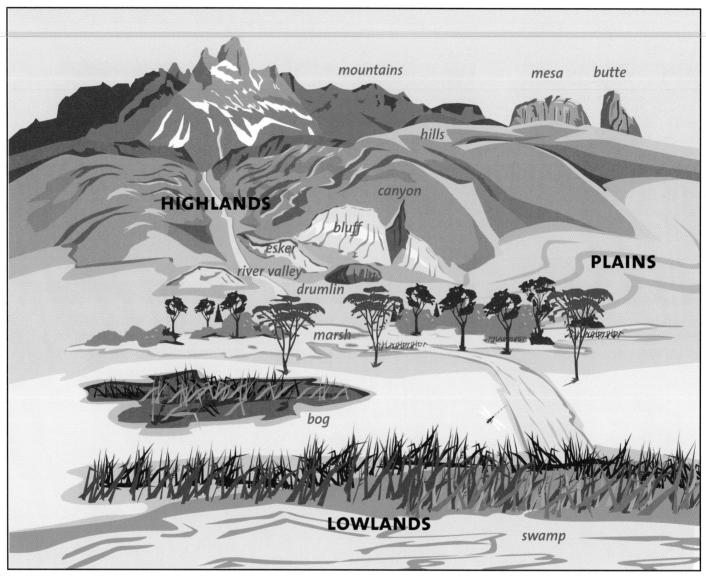

A composite landscape shows many kinds of landforms. (For definitions of the specific landforms, see Glossary, pp. 88–97.)

MOUNTAINS AND HIGHLANDS

A **mountain** is any point on land that rises quickly to at least 1,000 feet above its surroundings. Some mountains are jagged and snowcapped, and others are rounded and smooth. Some are volcanoes, with large craters in their tops.

Mountains exist below the oceans, too. Some of these mountains, while deep under the salty water, rise even higher than Mount Everest, the highest mountain on the continents.

A **hill** is an area on the earth's surface that rises above the land, but not more than 1,000 feet above the surrounding area. Any high land that is not a mountain can be classified as a hill. However, geologists and geographers have developed a special vocabulary for high landforms based on how the landforms were created.

PLAINS

Plains are large, flat, mostly treeless areas of land.

LOWLANDS

A **lowland** is an area of land that is lower than the land surrounding it. Just as geologists and geographers have a special vocabulary for highlands, they have a special vocabulary for lowlands.

A **valley** is a natural low place in the earth's surface, often located between mountains or hills. The bottom of a valley is called its **floor**, the sides its **walls**. A ridge between valleys is called a **divide**. Valleys with steep cliff walls are called **canyons** or **gorges**.

Other natural lowlands are **wetlands**, where the water level stays at or above the land's surface for most of the year. **Bogs**, **marshes**, and **swamps** are the most common types of wetlands.

> The study of the earth's physical features is called *geomorphology*.

Erosion and Weathering

Erosion is the gradual wearing away of land by the action of wind, water, or glaciers. **Weathering** is the gradual breakdown of rocks by weather, including wind, rain, snow, and changes in temperature (see p. 44). Erosion and weathering work together constantly to change the landforms on Earth.

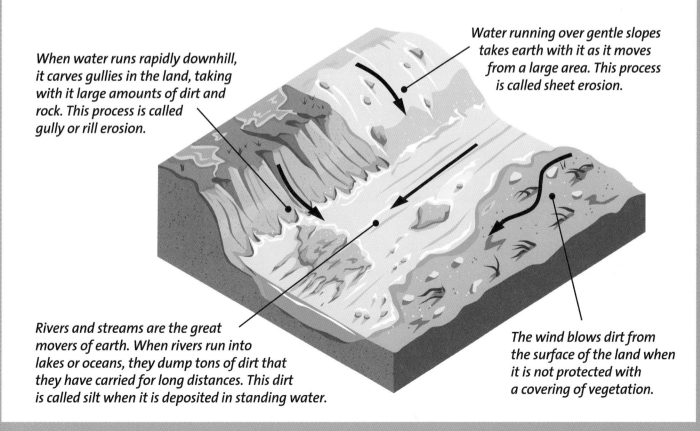

When water runs rapidly downhill, it carves gullies in the land, taking with it large amounts of dirt and rock. This process is called gully or rill erosion.

Water running over gentle slopes takes earth with it as it moves from a large area. This process is called sheet erosion.

Rivers and streams are the great movers of earth. When rivers run into lakes or oceans, they dump tons of dirt that they have carried for long distances. This dirt is called silt when it is deposited in standing water.

The wind blows dirt from the surface of the land when it is not protected with a covering of vegetation.

Glaciers

Glaciers are slow-moving sheets of ice found in high mountain valleys and polar regions. Glaciers cover about six million square miles, or three percent of the earth's surface.

Glaciers form at high latitudes and high elevations, where it is cold enough that more snow falls than melts or evaporates. Over the years, the snow gets deeper and deeper. Pressure from the weight of the snow finally turns the snow into huge sheets of ice. These ice sheets flow, like slow-moving rivers, down mountainsides until they reach warmer air along the oceans or at lower elevations. There the ice sheets melt or break off to form floating **icebergs**.

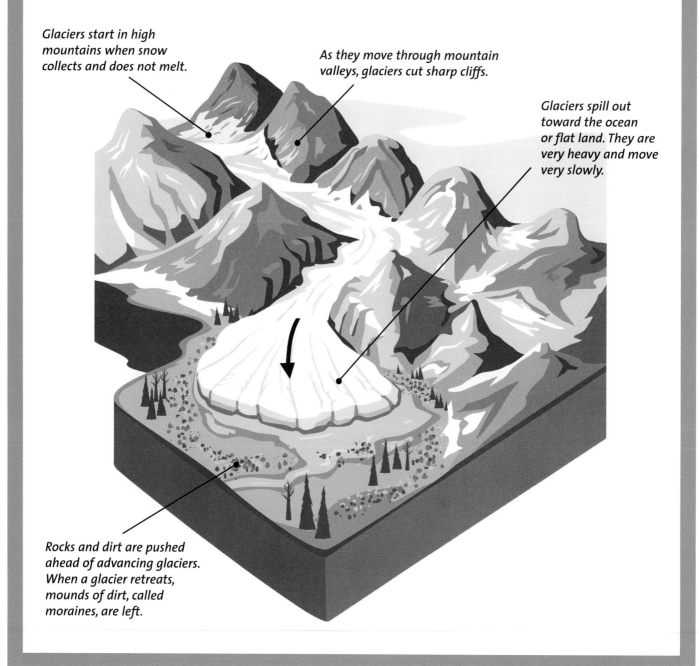

Glaciers start in high mountains when snow collects and does not melt.

As they move through mountain valleys, glaciers cut sharp cliffs.

Glaciers spill out toward the ocean or flat land. They are very heavy and move very slowly.

Rocks and dirt are pushed ahead of advancing glaciers. When a glacier retreats, mounds of dirt, called moraines, are left.

Chapter 2 The Water

Oceans

Oceans are large bodies of salt water that cover almost three-fourths of the earth's surface.

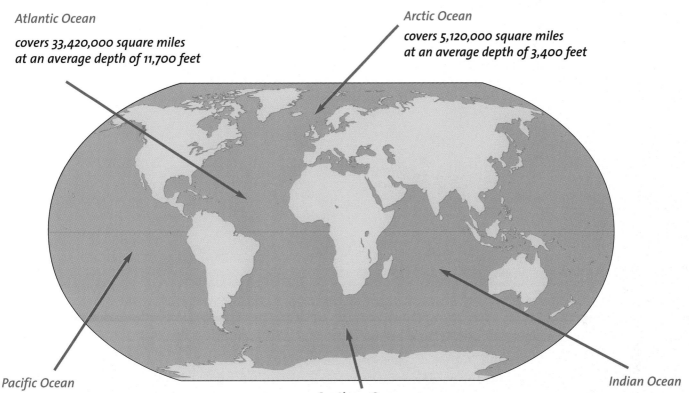

Atlantic Ocean
covers 33,420,000 square miles
at an average depth of 11,700 feet

Arctic Ocean
covers 5,120,000 square miles
at an average depth of 3,400 feet

Pacific Ocean
covers 64,200,000 square miles
at an average depth of 12,900 feet

Southern Ocean
covers 7,800,000 square miles
at an average depth of 14,750 feet

Indian Ocean
covers 28,400,000 square miles
at an average depth of 12,600 feet

The Briny Deep

	Depth (Feet)	Depth (Meters)		Depth (Feet)	Depth (Meters)
Pacific Ocean			**Indian Ocean**		
Mariana Trench	35,800	10,900	Java Trench	23,400	7,100
Tonga Trench	35,400	10,800	Ob' Trench	22,600	6,900
Philippine Trench	33,000	10,000	Diamantina Trench	21,700	6,600
Kermadec Trench	33,000	10,000	Vema Trench	21,000	6,400
Atlantic Ocean			**Arctic Ocean**		
Puerto Rico Trench	28,200	8,600	Eurasia Basin	17,900	5,500
South Sandwich Trench	27,300	8,300	**Southern Ocean**		
Cayman Trench	24,700	7,500	South Sandwich Trench	23,700	7,200
Romanche Gap	24,400	7,400			

The ocean floor, like the surface of the land, is made up of many features. Huge trenches drop off deeply from underwater plains. Plateaus and ridges rise thousands of feet to form mountains on the ocean floor. As on land, the underwater surface is formed by the movements of tectonic plates and shaped by the movement of water (see p. 31 and below).

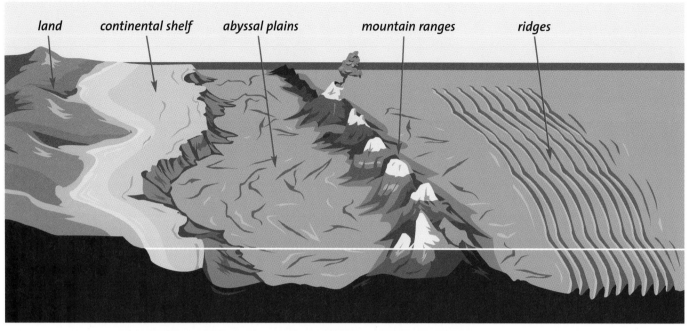

A cross section of the ocean floor shows some of the many features of its landscape.

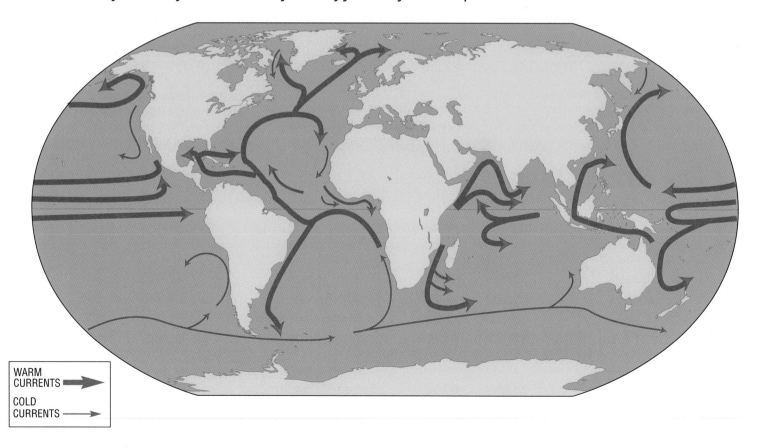

WARM CURRENTS →

COLD CURRENTS →

Ocean currents flow in predictable patterns throughout the major water bodies of the earth.

Natural Events Under Water

As on land, erosion, earthquakes, and volcanoes make regular changes under water.

In addition to changing the ocean floor, underwater volcanoes and earthquakes cause giant surges of water in the ocean. These surges of water may range from six to 60 feet high. When the surge of water, called a **tsunami**, hits land, it can cause dangerous flooding and wash away homes, roads, and buildings in its path.

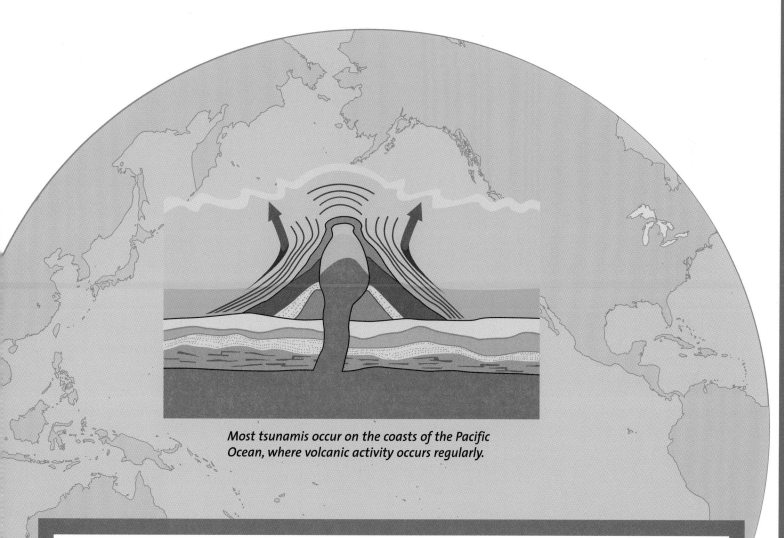

Most tsunamis occur on the coasts of the Pacific Ocean, where volcanic activity occurs regularly.

Tides

Tides are the daily changes in the levels of water in the oceans and seas. They are caused by the gravitational pull of the moon and sun on the earth. The moon affects tides more than the sun does. As the earth rotates on its axis, different parts of the earth face the moon (see pp. 13–14). The energy from gravity moves the water to the part of the ocean nearest the moon, where it piles up, or bulges. Oceans and seas on the opposite side of the earth bulge because of the way the earth spins. The bulges of water travel around the earth from east to west. They bring high tides to the oceans and seashores every 12 hours. When the bulge reaches a shore, it is high tide. When it is away from the shore, it is low tide.

Rivers

Rivers are bodies of water that begin at a source and flow downhill between banks of earth to a **mouth**, where they empty into a larger body of water. Most large rivers have three parts, or **courses**: **upper**, **middle**, and **estuary**.

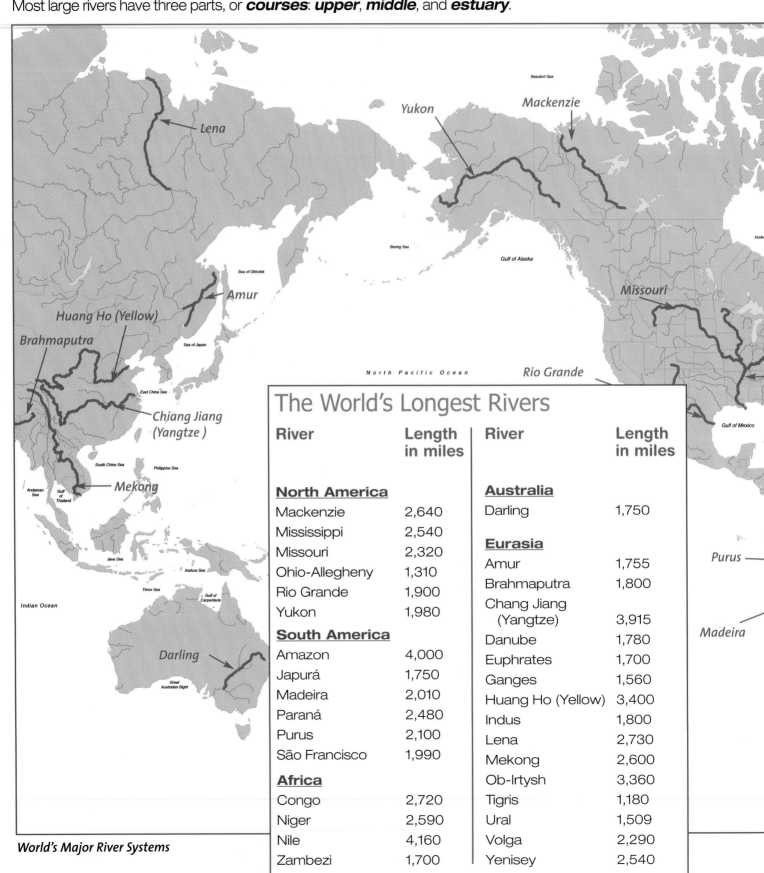

World's Major River Systems

The World's Longest Rivers

River	Length in miles	River	Length in miles
North America		**Australia**	
Mackenzie	2,640	Darling	1,750
Mississippi	2,540		
Missouri	2,320	**Eurasia**	
Ohio-Allegheny	1,310	Amur	1,755
Rio Grande	1,900	Brahmaputra	1,800
Yukon	1,980	Chang Jiang (Yangtze)	3,915
South America		Danube	1,780
Amazon	4,000	Euphrates	1,700
Japurá	1,750	Ganges	1,560
Madeira	2,010	Huang Ho (Yellow)	3,400
Paraná	2,480	Indus	1,800
Purus	2,100	Lena	2,730
São Francisco	1,990	Mekong	2,600
Africa		Ob-Irtysh	3,360
Congo	2,720	Tigris	1,180
Niger	2,590	Ural	1,509
Nile	4,160	Volga	2,290
Zambezi	1,700	Yenisey	2,540

Greenland Sea

Baffin Bay

Norwegian Sea

Yenisey

Labrador Sea

Gulf
of
Bothnia

Ob-Irtysh

North Sea

Baltic Sea

Volga

North Atlantic Ocean

English Channel

Ural

Bay of Biscay

Danube

Caspian Sea

Aral
Sea

Black Sea

Ohio-Allegheny

Tyrrhenian
Sea

Ganges

Ionian Sea

Mediterranean Sea

Tigris

Mississippi

Persian
Gulf

Gulf of Oman

Nile

Euphrates

Red
Sea

Arabian Sea

Bay of Bengal

Caribbean Sea

Indus

Japura

Amazon

São Francisco

Niger

Indian Ocean

Congo

South Atlantic Ocean

Parana

Zambezi

PARTS OF A RIVER

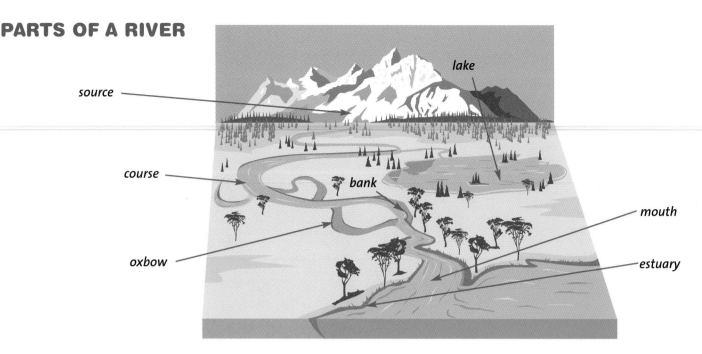

The source of the river shown here is melted water from a glacier, although rivers also form from the waters of highland springs and lakes flowing downhill, and from a combination of these waters. All rivers flow from a source to a mouth, where river waters empty into a larger body of water, sometimes another river, or a bay, gulf, lake, sea, or ocean. (For definitions of specific river parts, see Glossary, pp. 88–97.)

Seas, Gulfs, and Bays

Seas are large bodies of salt water or fresh water that are partly or completely enclosed by land. **Gulfs** and **bays** are large bodies of ocean or sea water that are partly surrounded by land. Bays are usually smaller than gulfs.

Lakes

Lakes are natural and human-made low spots on the land that have filled with water from flooding, melting glacial ice, rivers, and groundwater traveling downhill.

> Most lakes hold fresh water, although some hold salt water.
>
> **Ponds** are small lakes.

FOUR KINDS OF LAKES

Lakes can be divided into four types, depending on how they are formed.

CRATER LAKE

Water collects in craters left by volcanoes.

GLACIAL LAKE

Ice from glaciers carves depressions (low areas) in the landscape. The ice melts and forms a lake.

RIFT VALLEY LAKE

Shifts in plates on the earth's surface form depressions that fill with water.

ARTIFICIAL LAKE

Lakes are created artificially by building dams on rivers or by digging depressions and filling them with water from nearby sources.

Chapter 3

The Air: Atmosphere, Weather, and Climate

The Atmosphere

The **atmosphere** is the air that surrounds the earth. It is made up of five main layers. Although we don't pay much attention to the atmosphere most of the time, it is taller than any mountain, it extends past the horizon, and it is a very important element in the earth's geography. Without the atmosphere, the many variations in weather and climate that we know on the earth would not occur, and without those variations, different natural regions would not exist (see p. 50). Also, weather and climate affect the landforms physically through the processes of erosion and weathering (see p. 35).

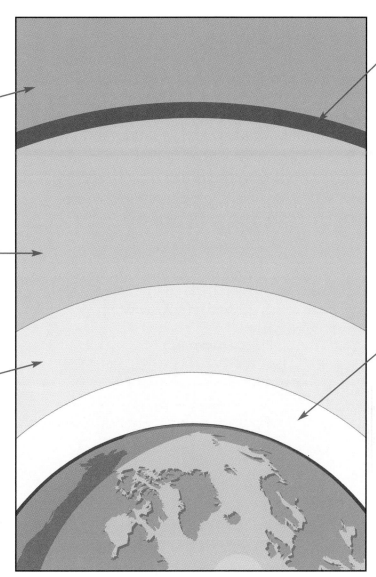

Thermosphere
Ranges to about 400 miles above the earth's surface. Within the thermosphere, electrically-charged particles called ions make up the ionosphere. Radio waves beamed up through the atmosphere bounce back to earth from the ion layers.

Exosphere
The border between the earth and space at about 310 miles. Satellites revolve around the earth in the exosphere.

Mesosphere
Ranges to about 50 miles. Temperatures drop to under −100°F.

Troposphere
About 12 miles thick at the equator and 5 miles thick at the poles. More than half the atmosphere's gases, water vapor, and dust particles are in the first 4 miles. We live here. Clouds and weather form here, too.

Stratosphere
Stretches to about 30 miles. Icy winds blow through the lower parts, speeding supersonic jets to their destinations. Above the clouds, the air is usually dry and clear. The ozone layer, which absorbs harmful ultraviolet rays from the sun, is here.

Weather and Climate

Weather is the day-to-day change in the atmosphere around us. The weather in a place varies constantly. It can be sunny and warm one day, cool and cloudy the next. Some days it rains, others it snows. Although many factors determine weather, two of the most important are temperature and precipitation (rain, snow, sleet, hail, or drizzle). The third most important factor is wind.

Climate is the usual weather in an area over a long period of time. Some words that describe different climates are *tropical, temperate,* and *arctic.* (See also Biomes, pp. 51–56).

HEAT

Most of the heat on Earth comes from the sun. (The rest radiates outward from the very hot interior of the earth.) The heat from the sun begins as sunlight passing through the atmosphere and being absorbed into the earth. It then changes to heat and rises from the surface of the earth to warm the atmosphere. This warming of the atmosphere near the earth's surface helps create wind systems and the patterns of weather.

The most important cause of weather is heat in the atmosphere. But not all sunlight that enters the earth's atmosphere is converted to heat. Some of the light is reflected back into space from the white tops of clouds and tiny particles of ice and water in the atmosphere. Some of the light reaches the surface of the earth and reflects off snow, water, and other reflective surfaces. Plants with green leaves absorb some of the light and change it into sugar and starch in the process called **photosynthesis**. The rest of the light is absorbed into the earth, converted into heat, and radiated back into the atmosphere, where its rising and cooling help create wind and weather.

> Dallol, Ethiopia, has the highest annual average temperature on Earth—94°F. Nedostupnosti Polyus, Antarctica, has the coldest annual average temperature— ⁻72°F. Nedostupnosti Polyus means "inaccessible pole."

AIR PRESSURE

The weight of the atmosphere pressing down on the earth is called **air pressure**. Because warm air is less dense than cold air, warm air forms areas of low air pressure and cold air forms areas of high pressure. High pressure usually means clear skies and sunny weather. Low pressure usually means cloudy, rainy, or snowy weather.

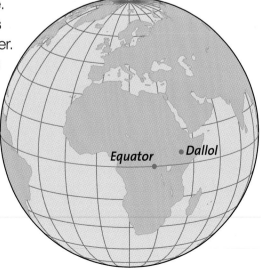

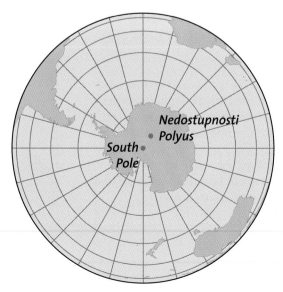

44

Weather Fronts

Cold Front
Cold air moves in on an area of warm air. The heavier cold air slides underneath the lighter warm air mass and pushes it up. **Clouds** and **thunderstorms** often form.

Warm Front
Warm air moves in on an area of cold air. The lighter warm air slides over the heavy, cold air, creating a front with a gentle slope. Clouds form, usually leading to some form of **precipitation**.

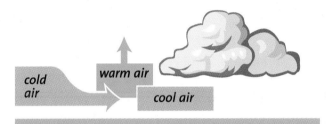

Stationary Front
Cold and warm air masses meet, but neither moves in on the other. Clouds often form at the boundary.

Occluded Fronts
When warm air is trapped between cold and cool air, it is forced upward. Clouds and precipitation usually result.

In places where the sun's rays reach the earth most directly and for the longest periods of time, the climate is warmer than in other places. Likewise, the coldest places are located where the sun's rays reach the earth less directly and for shorter periods of time.

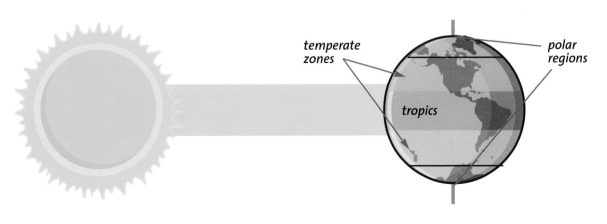

Water Heaters: Land and Ocean Temperatures

Oceans heat up more slowly than land masses. They also cool down more slowly. That means that in the summer the ocean is cooler than the land. It cools the air above it. This cool ocean air moves across the coastal land, keeping it cool. In winter, the water is warmer than the land, so the ocean air helps warm the air over coastal land. Temperatures vary less from summer to winter near oceans than they do in the middle of a continent.

In summer, the cooler water cools the air that moves from the sea to the coast.

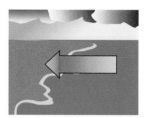

In winter, the warmer water warms the air that moves from the sea to the coast.

AIR

When air moves between areas of high and low pressure, **wind** results. The greater the difference in the pressure, the greater the speed of the wind. But air doesn't move in a straight line from one area to another. Instead, winds circle areas of high and low pressure, moving in opposite directions.

Warm air rises at the equator, and winds move in from north and south to take its place. The warm air cools and falls at around 30 degrees of latitude north and south, returning to the equator to replace other rising air. This circulation helps to cause similar air movements between 30 and 60 degrees latitude and between 60 degrees and the poles. The winds do not blow directly north and south because the earth's rotation skews them at an angle.

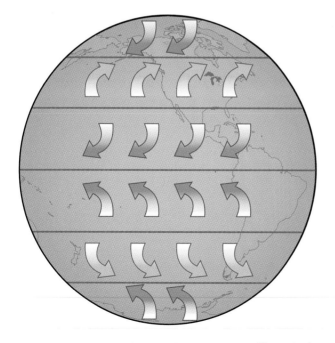
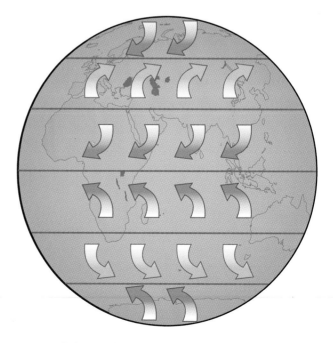

Prevailing wind patterns around the earth

HURRICANES, TORNADOES, TYPHOONS, AND CYCLONES

Hurricanes, *tornadoes*, *typhoons*, and *cyclones* are spirals of air moving around areas of intense low pressure.

Hurricanes are large storms that occur over water. These dangerous storms are known for their high winds that can topple trees and lift houses off their foundations. Hurricanes that affect the United States most often occur during the late summer and form in the Atlantic Ocean, Caribbean Sea, and Gulf of Mexico. The warm air circulating over the warm waters creates areas of low pressure. The winds surrounding the center, or eye, of the hurricane whip into speeds of 70 miles per hour and more. The eye remains calm. In countries bordering the Indian Ocean, hurricanes are called *cyclones*, although a cyclone means any large scale circular wind pattern that moves clockwise in the Southern Hemisphere and counterclockwise in the Northern Hemisphere. *Typhoon* is the name given to hurricanes that occur in the Pacific Ocean.

Tornadoes are spiral storms that occur only over land, most often forming over the Great Plains and in the upper Midwest of the United States from late spring until fall.

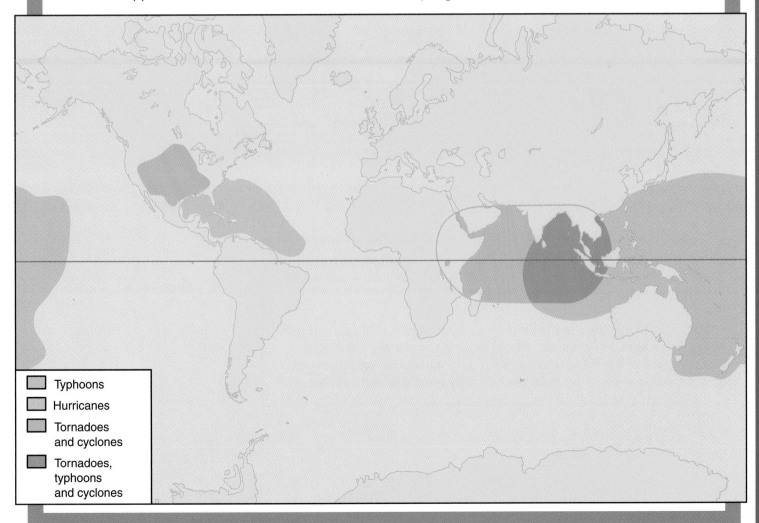

Typhoons

Hurricanes

Tornadoes and cyclones

Tornadoes, typhoons and cyclones

Water in the Air

Water and heat work together to create different weather conditions. Heat warms water in lakes, rivers, and oceans. The water **evaporates**, or changes from liquid to a gas called ***water vapor***. Water vapor cools and condenses into droplets in the atmosphere to form clouds, fog, or ice crystals. These droplets grow heavier and fall back to the earth in the form of precipitation—rain, snow, sleet, hail, or drizzle. Warm air can hold more water vapor than cold air. That means that the humidity—or the amount of water vapor in the air—is usually greater on warm days than on cold ones.

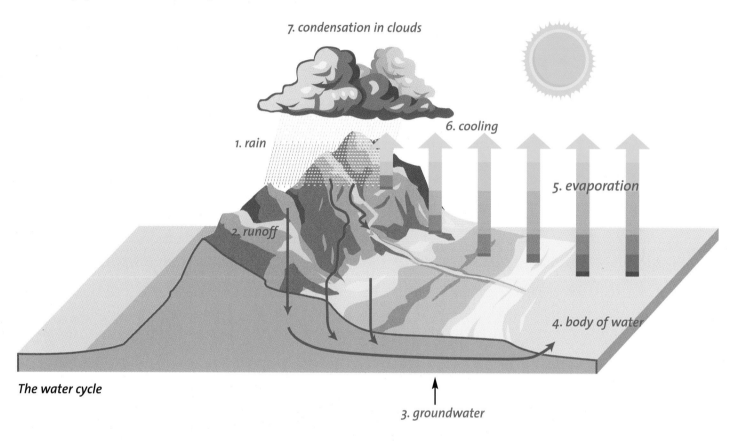

7. condensation in clouds

1. rain

6. cooling

5. evaporation

2. runoff

4. body of water

3. groundwater

The water cycle

On any day, about four trillion (4,000,000,000,000) gallons of water—about ten times the amount of water in all the world's rivers—are in the atmosphere in the form of water vapor.

The amount of moisture in the air is called *humidity*. Humidity is referred to in percentages. For example, when the air is completely filled with water vapor, the humidity is 100 percent. When the air is holding about half the water vapor it can hold, the humidity is measured at 50 percent.

Insulation: CLOUDS AND CLIMATE

Insulation prevents heat from passing into or out of an area. Your coat insulates your body, keeping your body heat in. The thick walls of a refrigerator keep the cold air inside and prevent the warm air outside from getting in.

Clouds insulate the earth. During the day they act as shields reflecting the sun's light and keep much of it from reaching the surface of the earth. At night, they act as blankets, reflecting heat leaving the earth's surface downward again. So cloudy skies tend to bring smaller swings of temperature from day to night than clear skies.

Winds at Sea

The warm and cold winds that blow across the earth don't just move air. They also push surface water along as waves. These become ocean currents, some warm and others cold. Warm and cold currents, like winds, affect the weather and climate in different places on the earth. (See also ocean currents map, p. 38.)

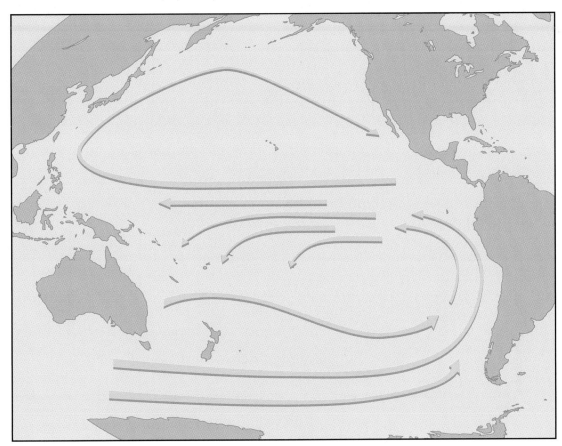

This map shows the pattern of winds over the Pacific Ocean.

The Natural Regions of the World

Chapter 1

Land Biomes

The earth can be divided into about ten different natural regions, or **land biomes**. Each biome is unique, with a special mixture of physical features—landforms, bodies of water, and climate—and their own forms of plant and animal life.

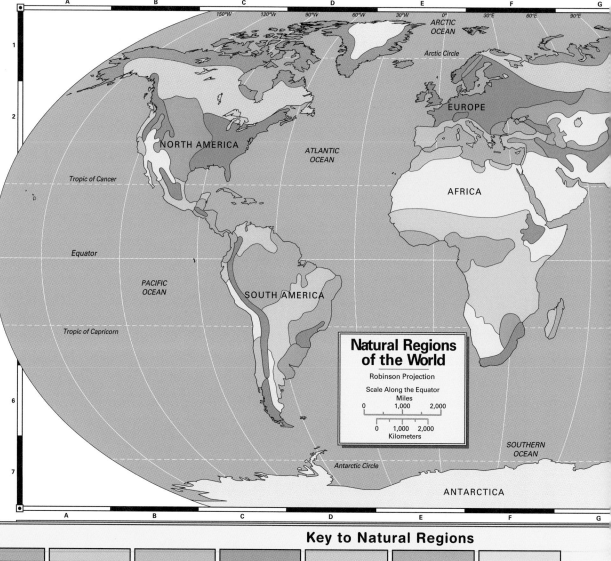

Natural Regions of the World

Robinson Projection

Scale Along the Equator
Miles
0   1,000   2,000

0   1,000   2,000
Kilometers

Key to Natural Regions

Tropical Rain Forest
Thick trees, mostly with broad leaves that stay green all year; hot and wet year-round

Tropical Grassland
Some trees among tall grasses; hot with both wet and dry seasons

Mediterranean
Wide open forests, some clumps of trees; many shrubs, herbs, and grasses; hot, dry summers, cool-to-mild winters

Temperate Forest
Mixed forests; trees that lose their leaves in winter; also trees with needles that stay green year-round; cool to cold in winter, warm in summer

Cool Forest
Mostly trees with needles that stay green year-round; some trees that lose their leaves in winter; long, cold winters, cool-to-mild summers

Cool Grassland
Prairies with tall, thick grasses and higher lands with shorter grass; cool in winter, warm in summer; drier than forest regions

Desert
Sand or completely bare soil; very few plants; in some areas, patches of grass, cactus, and bushes; very little rain

Chapter 2 The Biomes

Tropical Rain Forests

Tropical rain forests are warm, wet biomes near or at the equator, where more species of plants and animals flourish than in all other biomes combined.

Hundreds of varieties of trees grow in tropical rain forests, most of them hardwoods. Although the warm, wet conditions encourage luxurious growth, the trees grow so close together that they have to fight for the light they need to grow. To catch more light, trees grow very tall, and the upper branches spread out over a wide area. The tops of trees grow close together, weaving a thick layer of leaves and branches called the forest canopy. The canopy is so thick that little sunlight gets through to the rain forest floor. Between the canopy and the floor grows a layer of shrubs and small trees that rises about ten to 50 feet above the floor. This layer is called the understory. Some trees are very tall, and their branches and leaves tower at the top of the canopy. These are emergent trees, and are usually hardwoods, such as mahogany, rosewood, and ebony.

Because the floor of the rain forest is dark and damp, plants that require sunlight do not grow quickly. The few plants that grow there have broad, flat leaves to absorb as much sunlight as possible. Their leaves have waxy surfaces and pointed tips to allow water to run off easily. Other plants along the floor include vines that grow on top of understory shrubs and up tree trunks toward the light in the canopy.

Plant life is richer in the canopy than on the floor, as is the animal life. Reptiles, amphibians, birds, and mammals live together in the treetops of the rain forest. These tree-dwelling, or *arboreal*, animals include frogs, snakes, termites, eagles, toucans, parrots, flying squirrels, leopards, bats, and monkeys.

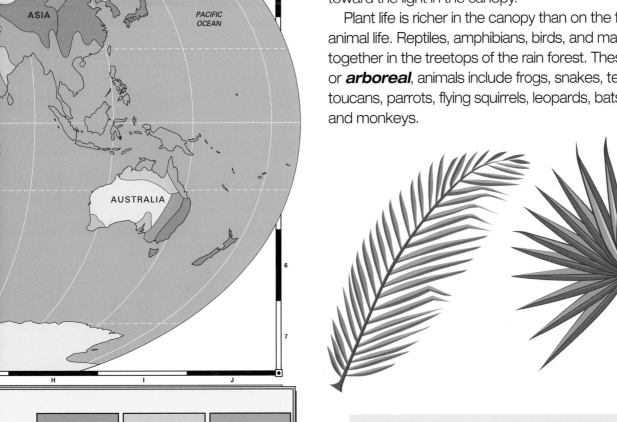

Tundra	Arctic	High Mountain
Rolling plains with no trees; patches of short grass, moss, and small flowering plants	Frozen desert, covered with ice all year; no plant life	Many different climates, depending on location; can have tropical forests at the bottom; cool forests in the middle; cold tundra higher up; snow and ice at the top

Average Daytime Temperature: 80° F
Average Nighttime Temperature: 70° F
Average Annual Rainfall: 100–200 inches

Tropical Grasslands

Tropical grasslands, often called **savannas**, are biomes located inland at or near the equator.

The seasons in tropical grasslands are called the wet season and the dry season. Because it's hot year-round, the seasons are determined by variations in rainfall, not temperature.

Few plants survive here except for tough grasses and a few hardy types of trees, among them baobabs and acacia, which have thick trunks, deep roots, and waxy, spiny leaves. These features allow them to survive the extreme drought of the dry season.

The thick grasses are food to the millions of savanna animals, among them antelopes, wildebeests, zebras, giraffes, gazelles, rhinos, buffalos, and elephants. Enormous herds of these grazers roam up and down the grasslands following the rains and searching for water and fresh grasses. Other animals, including cheetahs, leopards, and lions, follow the grazers to prey on them. Still others, including hyenas and jackals, scavenge the remains of dead or dying animals. The savannas also support hundreds of species of birds, from tiny sunbirds to eagles, and unique reptiles, amphibians, and insects.

Average Daytime Temperature: 80°F
Average Nighttime Temperature: 55°F
Average Annual Rainfall: 10–40 inches

Mediterranean Regions

Mediterranean regions, also called **chaparrals**, are coastal biomes that are cool and moist in the winter and hot and dry in the summer. These biomes support clumps of trees and some widely spread forests.

During hot summer months, drought-resistant evergreens prove the hardiest plants in this scrubland and grass biome. The leaves and stems provide moisture and nutrition for a variety of animals, most of them small enough to seek cover beneath the low branches as they nibble on leaves. Here is a home for rodents—tiny mice and rabbits—and their predators. Underground or deep in shade, lizards wait out the heat of the day. Foxes and hawks, and other predator mammals and birds, stalk and circle to make a meal of the small local fare.

The chaparral is different in winter months, when it is cooler and wetter. Then plants grow more abundantly and the animal populations surge as well. Even large grazers, such as deer, gather to nibble on the winter foliage.

Average Daytime Temperature:
90°F summer, 55°F winter
Average Nighttime Temperature:
70°F summer, 40°F winter
Average Annual Rainfall: about 10 inches

Temperate Forests

In the areas between the cold polar regions and the hot tropics of both hemispheres are **temperate forests** with warm summers and cool winters.

These temperate forests are dominated by deciduous trees, such as oak, elm, ash, maple, and birch. Evergreens are also present in these forests, including the giant sequoias of the temperate forests in northern California.

In spring and summer, the leaves of the trees provide shade for the forest floor, so temperatures remain cool. Although winters can be cold—often below freezing—the forest remains an inviting environment for many types of plants and animals, from earthworms and insects to songbirds, predator birds, deer, and foxes.

Average Daytime Temperature:
68°F summer, 32°F winter
Average Nighttime Temperature:
58°F summer, 18°F winter
Average Annual Rainfall: about 40 inches

Cool Forests

Also called **boreal** forests, **cool forests** are made up mostly of coniferous (cone-bearing) trees. The conifers grow better than other trees in these cold regions located in the extreme temperate zones and into the polar regions, where summer is short and winter is long and dark. Pine, spruce, and hemlock trees grow here, supplying cover to a few year-round residents, including birds; small mammals such as rodents, rabbits, and squirrels; and large animals such as moose, elk, caribou, and bears.

In the winter, the boreal residents tuck themselves away into natural shelters; many graze only an hour or two each day in the freezing temperatures, others hibernate during the months of deepest chill.

But spring brings summer a full complement of migratory animals, particularly birds, who seek the mild summer temperatures and abundant food in the cool forest. These animals will stay until, as summer turns to autumn, instinct tells them to move back to their tropical winter homes.

Average Daytime Temperature:
65°F summer, 20°F winter
Average Nighttime Temperature:
50°F summer, 10°F winter
Average Annual Rainfall: about 20 inches

Cool Grasslands

Cool grasslands include **prairies** covered in tall grasses and other regions with shorter grasses. These grasslands are drier than cool forest regions, but experience similar summer and winter temperatures.

Few of the cool grassland biomes have been left in their natural state by human beings. That's because the grasslands are excellent for farming both livestock and crops.

Instead of serving as natural grazing lands for large herds of wild animals, the grasslands are now covered in soybeans, wheat, barley, oats, and other grain crops. Populations of cows, sheep, horses, goats, and other domesticated animals feed on the coarse grasses.

> Average Daytime Temperature: 75°F summer, 20°F winter
> Average Nighttime Temperature: 60°F summer, 0°F winter
> Average Annual Rainfall: under 25 inches

Deserts

Deserts are regions—hot or cold—where the land is covered in sand or bare soil and precipitation totals are very small, less than ten inches each year.

In most hot deserts, temperatures vary greatly, from extremely hot days to cool, even freezing, nights.

Plant and animal life in deserts is well adapted to the harsh environment. Cacti and euphorbia are typical desert plants. Called **succulents**, these plants store water in their waxy leaves and stems. To avoid the hot days, many animals in the desert are **nocturnal**, or active only at night. These animals burrow deep into the earth to spend the daylight hours away from the burning sun. They search for food during the cool nighttime hours. Certain types of lizards and snakes thrive in the hot desert sun, as do animals that need only a little water.

Although we often think of deserts as hot places, not all deserts are hot. The far north of Siberia in Russia and much of Antarctica are cold deserts.

> Average Daytime Temperature: 100°F summer, 65°F winter*
> Average Nighttime Temperature: 75°F summer, 45°F winter*
> Average Annual Rainfall: under 10 inches

*Averages represent hot deserts located in tropical and temperate regions, not frozen deserts.

Tundra

Tundra biomes are extreme climates, too cold for trees to grow. While the top of the ground thaws during the warm season, a layer beneath it, about ten inches of frozen ground, never melts. It is called **permafrost**.

In this harsh biome, winter is particularly cruel. Yet a few animals remain after the others have migrated south for the winter. Lemmings, ermines, arctic foxes, wolves, musk oxen, reindeer, and polar bears grow heavy winter coats or huddle into dens to keep warm through the long, dark winter.

During the few short months of warm weather, low-growing tundra flowers bloom. Birds and insects newly arrived from the south feast on these, as do herds of moose and caribou that have traveled to the tundra from their winter homes farther south.

Average Daytime Temperature: 55°F summer, 30°F winter
Average Nighttime Temperature: 40°F summer, −10°F winter
Average Annual Rainfall: 30–45 inches

Polar Regions

The **polar regions** are frozen deserts covered in ice all year long. Because it is over land instead of water, the Antarctic is much colder than the Arctic.

The Arctic polar region (around the north pole) is a solid mass of frozen ocean water. The Antarctic polar region (around the south pole) is a mass of frozen land covered in ice and snow. Together, the areas surrounding the north and south poles are known as the **polar ice caps**.

Powerful icy winds blow across the polar ice caps, causing blizzards of snow and ice blown up from the surface. However, little snow actually falls from the skies over the ice caps because the air temperatures are too cold for moisture to evaporate and form clouds.

Only migrating animals, such as polar bears and arctic seals, are found on the Arctic ice mass. Very few animals are hearty enough to survive conditions in Antarctica. The few that do manage it live along the coasts of the continent, relying upon the sea for food and shelter. Among these remarkable animals are such birds as petrels, gulls, terns, albatrosses, and penguins. Penguins are insulated with a heavy coat of feathers over skin protected by a thick layer of fat.

In the icy north arctic seas live Arctic mammals. Here dolphins, porpoises, whales, and seals, protected by thick layers of oily fat called **blubber**, swim in the near-freezing waters.

Average Daytime Temperature:	Arctic: 30°F summer, −10°F winter
	Antarctic: 7°F summer, −80°F winter
Average Nighttime Temperature:	Arctic: 10°F summer, −20°F winter
	Antarctic: −50°F summer, −95°F winter
Average Annual Rainfall:	5–20 inches

Mountain Biomes

Because of the changes in altitude (height above sea level), high mountain environments support a variety of different climates. Depending on the location of the mountain ranges, biomes on high mountains can range from tropical rain forest to tundra and frozen desert. Mountains also help create different biomes. As warm, moist air flows from coastal regions up against mountain ranges on their **windward** sides, the air pushes upward and cools. The cooled water vapor condenses into droplets in the form of clouds. Often these droplets become large enough to fall as rain. Because moisture-carrying air is blocked by the mountain ranges, drier climates, such as plains or deserts, often form on the **leeward** sides.

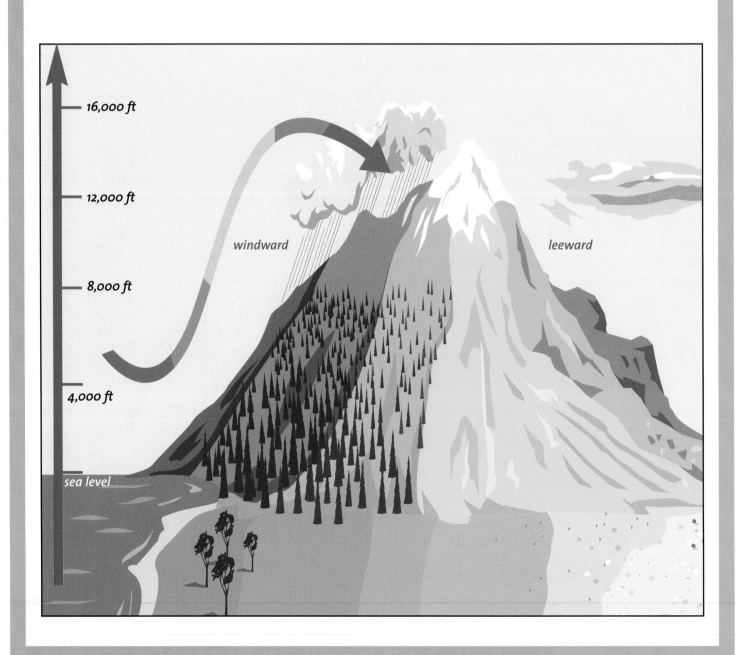

People on Land and Water

Chapter 1

Location and Place

What Are Location and Place?

Location is where something—for example, a house, a school, a store, an airport, a mine, or a crop field—is created or built. Location is described in absolute terms (latitude and longitude) or relative terms (north of the road or near the playground). A location becomes a **place** when it is described in terms of its human or physical characteristics.

Climate and landscape, as well as religion, schools, politics, opportunities to make a living, and environmental surroundings give character to a place.

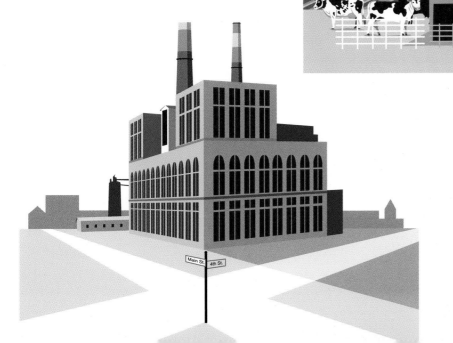

A farm and a factory are two kinds of places. Farms are usually located in the countryside. The factory on the left is located at the intersection of 4th and Main streets.

Population

Population is the total number of people who live in a particular place. Geographers study population to understand where people live and why they live there.

WORLD POPULATION GROWTH

Key
- ■ Decreasing
- □ Stable growth
- ▨ Above average growth

Drawn from data collected from the U.S. Bureau of the Census International Database

A map of world population growth shows areas where the number of people is growing, decreasing, or remaining about the same.

> The study of population is called *demographics*.
> Scientists who study demographics are called *demographers*.

WORLD POPULATION GROWTH, 1600–PRESENT

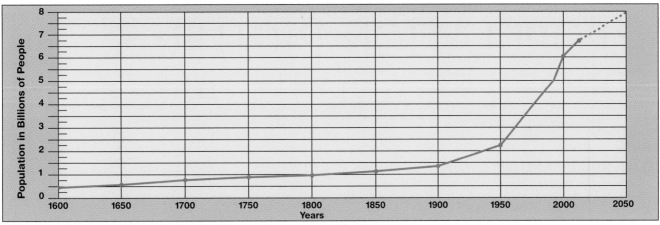

This graph shows world population in billions of people over the last 400 years.

Population Data

In studying human populations, geographers use a lot of different information called **population data**. These data include basic facts about human populations—past, present, and projected into the future.

SOME TYPES OF POPULATION DATA

1 **Average family size** — The average number of children in a family in a particular culture group or region

2 **Birth rate** — The number of babies born per year per thousand people

3 **Death rate** — The number of people who die per year per thousand people

4 **Doubling time** — The time needed for a population to increase 100 percent (double)

5 **Life expectancy** — The average number of years people live

6 **Population growth rate** — How quickly a population grows each year, measured by percentage

7 **Population structure** — The makeup of a population by age and gender (male or female)

> The world's population increases by about three people every second. That's nearly 200 people a minute, 10,000 people an hour, and 240,000 people a day!

POPULATION PICTURES: PROFILES AND PYRAMIDS

Geographers use graphs to compare populations in different areas. Two of the most common graphs are the **population profile** and the **population pyramid**.

POPULATION PROFILE

A **population profile** is a bar graph that shows the different age groups of a population that share something in common, such as language, dog ownership, or a school.

POPULATION PYRAMID

A **population pyramid** is a bar graph that depicts a total population by breaking it down into age groupings and gender.

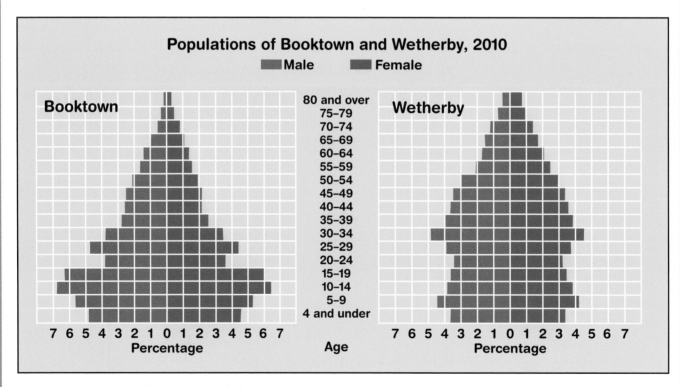

By comparing the population pyramids for Booktown and Wetherby, you can see that a larger percentage of Booktown is aged 10–19 than Wetherby. That is because the Boys' Academy of Reading, an all-male middle and high school, brings hundreds of school-age boys into Booktown each year, skewing the population in that age group.

Population Density and Distribution

Population density means how close together people live in a particular place. To find population density, divide the number of people in a place by the total area of that place.

   Population distribution or **patterns** tell geographers where most people live within a place or region.

Maps show both population density and distribution. This map shows the population density and distribution in the state of Wisconsin. More than half of the 5,600,000 residents live in cities located in the southeastern and south central parts of the state. Located in these areas are the largest cities in the state: Milwaukee, Madison, and Green Bay.

WISCONSIN POPULATION DENSITY AND DISTRIBUTION

• *Green Bay*
(app. population 101,000)

⭐ *Madison*
(app. population 235,000)

• *Milwaukee*
(app. population 605,000)

Drawn from data gathered by the U.S. Bureau of the Census

Persons per square mile

More than 100

50 to 100

25 to 50

less than 25

Urban vs. Rural

About half the earth's people live in cities and towns, called **urban areas**.
The other half live on farms or in countryside villages, called **rural areas**.

POPULATION PATTERNS: URBAN VS. RURAL

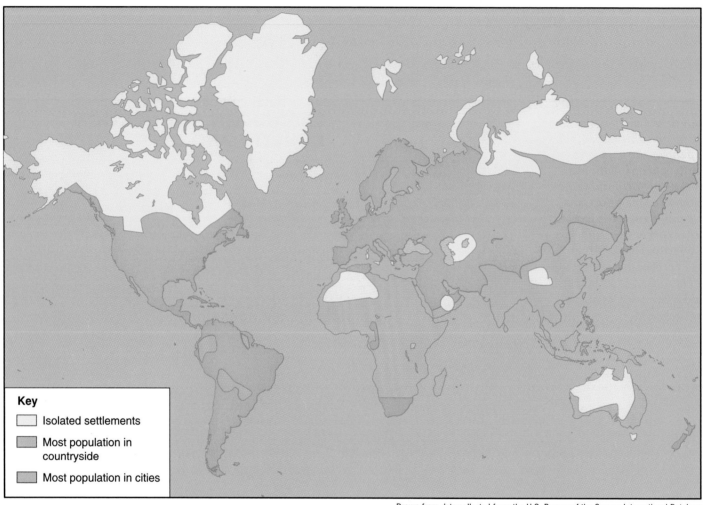

Key
- Isolated settlements
- Most population in countryside
- Most population in cities

Drawn from data collected from the U.S. Bureau of the Census International Database

*A map of population patterns shows where people live mostly in cities
(urban) and where people live mostly in the countryside (rural).*

A MODEL CITY, A MODEL COUNTRYSIDE

A **city**, or **metropolis**, is a large or important town. Sometimes a city grows so large that it grows into a neighboring city, forming a **megalopolis**. But no matter how big it is, a city is made up of a variety of areas.

Businesses and industries are located in the **commercial areas** of a city. Stores and service businesses often are located in **downtown** commercial areas, or the main business area of a city, called the **central business district (CBD)**. Manufacturing and heavy industry (see p. 75) are usually located along the outer edges of a city on major transportation routes (roads, waterways, trains, airports, etc.).

People's homes are located in the **residential** areas of a city. Homes are also found in the **suburbs**, or the residential districts lying just outside a city or town. Like the people who live in the residential areas of a city, people who live in the suburbs usually work in the city and benefit from the services the city offers. Beyond the suburbs are **exurbs**, sparsely populated residential areas.

Most cities are divided into **neighborhoods**, each with its own special cultural makeup. Some neighborhoods are made up of people with the same ethnic or religious background. For example, many U.S. cities have Chinese, Italian, Korean, or African-American neighborhoods. Other neighborhoods are unique because of their architecture or the era in which they were built. Many U.S. cities have preserved their "historic districts" or the "old cities" where the oldest buildings in the city stand. Still other neighborhoods are defined by physical features. Terms such as "riverside," "highlands," and "flats" are often used to describe neighborhoods within cities.

Outside cities are small towns, villages, and other rural communities, as well as farmland, forests, parks, and other tracts of land. Highways, smaller roads, waterways, railroads, and other transportation routes connect rural areas to each other and to nearby cities, states, or even foreign countries.

> **Towns** are usually smaller than cities, but both are thickly populated areas with fixed boundaries and local governments.

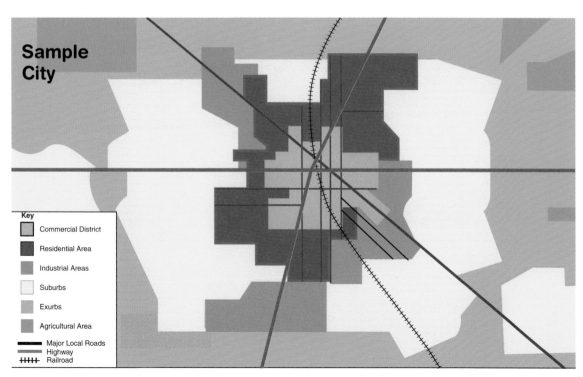

Sample City

Like most cities, Sample City is made up of several distinct areas, including a downtown, industrial district, residential neighborhoods, and suburbs.

Key
- Commercial District
- Residential Area
- Industrial Areas
- Suburbs
- Exurbs
- Agricultural Area
- Major Local Roads
- Highway
- Railroad

World Birth Rates: 1910–2010

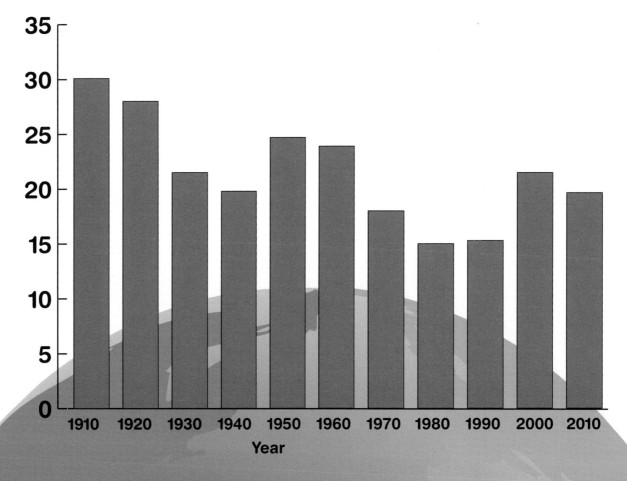

Rate of Births
(per 1,000 people per year)

Chapter 3 Culture

What Is Culture?

Culture is a word used to describe how groups of people act: how we live, what we eat, what we believe, and how we change our environment to create communities.

Geographers who study culture try to explain how people behaved in the past compared with how we behave today. They compare the way people in different areas live their lives. They study languages, beliefs and traditions, political systems, and the technologies that bind communities together or make them different from other communities.

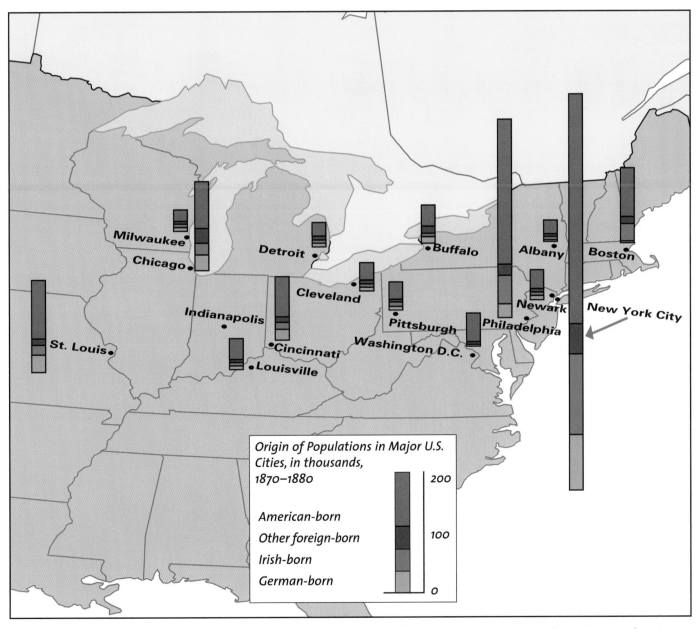

Origin of Populations in Major U.S. Cities, in thousands, 1870–1880

200

American-born

Other foreign-born

100

Irish-born

German-born

0

This cultural map compares the Irish and German populations to other foreign-born and American-born citizens of major northeastern and midwestern American cities in the 1870s.

THE CULTURAL MOSAIC

Geographers consider each culture group to consist of different pieces, like the pieces in a **mosaic**, a picture made by fitting together separate tiles, stones, or glass pieces. Viewed together, the pieces that make up a culture create a picture of that culture, called a **cultural mosaic**.

Elements of the cultural mosaic can be witnessed in a typical American suburban backyard. The types of clothes we wear, the food we eat, the games we play, and the architecture of our homes are all pieces of our cultural mosaic.

Culture Basics

1. **Language** (see below)

2. **Beliefs and traditions** (see pp. 68–70)

3. **Arts and crafts** (see p. 71)

4. **Political systems** (see p. 74)

5. **Technologies** (see p. 75)

Language

Language is the use of voice sounds, gestures, and written symbols to communicate thoughts and feelings.

> **The five languages most widely spoken in the world today are Mandarin Chinese, English, Hindi, Spanish, and Russian.**

LANGUAGE FAMILIES

More than 2,800 languages are spoken in the world today. These languages have been grouped into several **language families**. Here are some of the main groups.

FAMILY/GROUP	PRINCIPAL LANGUAGES
Afro-Asian	Amharic, Arabic, Berber, Hebrew
Black African	Includes Khoisan, Niger-Kordofanian, and Nilo-Saharan language families
Dravidian	Tamil, Telugu
Indo-European	Albanian, Armenian, Belorussian, Bengali, Bulgarian, Croatian, Czech, Danish, Dutch, English, French, German, Greek, Gujarati, Hindi, Icelandic, Iranian, Italian, Latvian, Lithuanian, Macedonian, Marathi, Norwegian, Polish, Portuguese, Punjabi, Romanian, Russian, Serbian, Slovak, Slovenian, Spanish, Swedish, Ukrainian, Urdu
Korean and Japanese	Korean and Japanese
Malayo-Polynesian	Indonesian, Malagasy, Malay, Maori, Pilipino, Tagalog
Mon-Khmer	Khmer and Laotian
Sino-Tibetan	Burmese, Chinese, Lao, Tibetan, Thai, Vietnamese
Uralic-Altaic	Estonian, Finnish, Hungarian, Turkish

> **Slang** is a variation of language used instead of standard vocabulary. It is usually used to provide emphasis or humor in speech and, sometimes, in writing. A **dialect** is a variation of a standard language spoken by a particular group of people. A dialect differs from standard language in grammar, vocabulary, or pronunciation, or in any combination of the three.

LANGUAGE BARRIERS

Throughout early history, mountains stopped the spread of language. So did large bodies of water, deserts, and thick jungles. Because people couldn't cross these barriers easily, groups of people on opposite sides developed languages separately. So, people on one side of a geographic barrier might speak a language different from people on the other. Today these boundaries are no longer difficult to cross, yet they help explain the diversity of world languages.

> More than 1,000 Native American languages are spoken in isolated areas throughout the Americas.

WORLD LANGUAGE FAMILIES

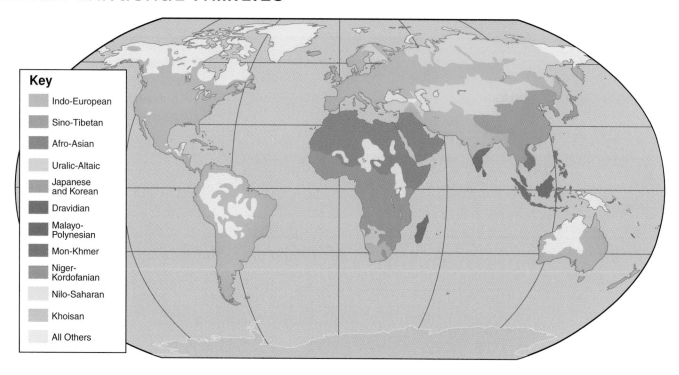

Key
- Indo-European
- Sino-Tibetan
- Afro-Asian
- Uralic-Altaic
- Japanese and Korean
- Dravidian
- Malayo-Polynesian
- Mon-Khmer
- Niger-Kordofanian
- Nilo-Saharan
- Khoisan
- All Others

Beliefs and Traditions: Religions, Customs, and Arts and Crafts

Beliefs are the attitudes, ideas, and world views held by a person or a group of people. Every culture has a set of beliefs, or a **belief system**. This system is made up of three basic elements:

1 Religion — A belief in and legends about a god or gods who created the world and affect peoples' lives

2 Customs and manners — The traditions people have or ways people act or behave in a group

3 Arts and crafts — The clothing, music, arts, architecture, tools, etc., used by a group

RELIGION

Over the centuries, people have believed in many religions. Today, dozens of religions are practiced in the world. However, five major religions are the most widely practiced.

MAJOR WORLD RELIGIONS (In order of approximate date of origin)

1 Hinduism — Begun about 1500 B.C. in India. Hindus believe in many gods and in reincarnation (rebirth of the soul after death). Today, Hinduism is practiced by 900 million people primarily in India, Nepal, Malaysia, Indonesia, Guyana, Suriname, and Sri Lanka.

2 Judaism — Begun about 1300 B.C. among the Hebrew people in the Middle East. Judaism was the first religion founded on a belief in one god rather than a group of gods. Today, Judaism is practiced by 14 million people throughout the world, primarily in Israel, Europe, and the United States.

3 Buddhism — Begun about 525 B.C. by Siddhartha Gautama (Buddha), c. 563–480, in India. Buddhists follow the Hindu belief in reincarnation, and they work to gain inner peace, called nirvana. Today, Buddhism is practiced by approximately 360 million people throughout Asia, from Sri Lanka to Japan.

4 Christianity — Begun in the first century in the Middle East among Jews who believed that Jesus of Nazareth was the divine son of god. Today, Christianity is practiced by approximately 2 billion people throughout the world, primarily in Europe, North America, South America, and Africa, as well as in pockets of Asia.

5 Islam — Begun in A.D. 622 in the Middle East by followers of Muhammad. Islam includes many of the features of Judaism and Christianity, including the belief in one god, which Moslems call Allah. Today, Islam is practiced by 1.3 billion people, primarily in the western and northern countries of Africa, throughout the Middle East, and in Central Asia, western China, Malaysia, Indonesia, the Philippines, and the United States.

The rest of the world's population, approximately 1.8 billion people, practices other religions or no religion.

CUSTOMS AND MANNERS

Customs are the usual habits of a group of people. **Manners**, or norms, are the habits considered to be polite among a group of people. Both customs and manners are the result of what a group considers important: its values. For example, when a young person offers a seat to an older person, the custom demonstrates the value of respect for one's elders.

GREETINGS!
Manners, Meanings, and Cultural Differences

What is accepted as polite behavior in one place isn't necessarily so in another.

Waving with the palm of the hand facing out is a gesture of greeting in America and most European cultures. In Turkey and Greece, however, the gesture is called "The Hand of Moutza," and is considered a serious insult.

In the United States, people often shake hands as a greeting or when they are introduced to new people. In Japan and India, touch is not used in greetings. In Japan, people bow to acknowledge new contacts or to express respect to old friends. In India, people touch their palms together, prayer-style, to show welcome.

Sticking out the tongue is considered rude in the United States, but among the Aborigines in Australia, it is a sign of greeting and affection. In China, it is a sign of embarrassment.

ARTS AND CRAFTS

Art communicates the values and beliefs of a culture in what that culture finds beautiful. It can include paintings, sculpture, plays, poems, dance, photographs, movies, novels, and music.

Crafts refers to useful items and the methods used to make them. Crafts include sewing, weaving, tools for cooking, farming, mining, manufacturing, and the design and construction of buildings (architecture).

> All the art forms—visual arts, music, literature, and dance—together are called the fine arts.

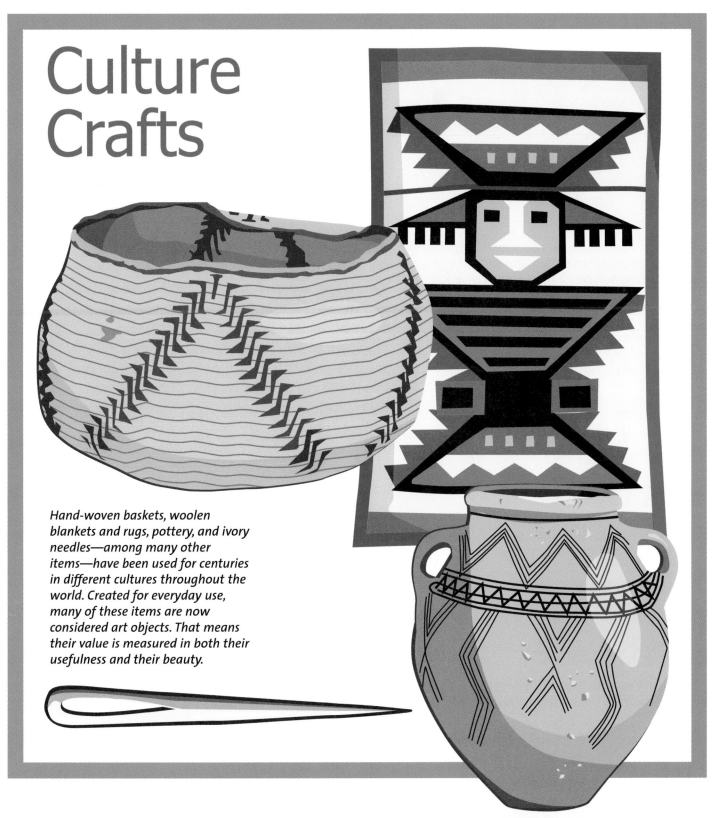

Culture Crafts

Hand-woven baskets, woolen blankets and rugs, pottery, and ivory needles—among many other items—have been used for centuries in different cultures throughout the world. Created for everyday use, many of these items are now considered art objects. That means their value is measured in both their usefulness and their beauty.

HOME SWEET HOME
The Architecture of Houses

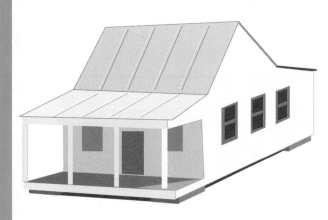

Plantation-style houses have been built around the world by European settlers. This particular style of house, however, is most often seen in agricultural or tropical regions.

Teepees were once home to some of the members of the Plains nations of Native Americans.

People in different cultural groups tend to build different kinds of houses. The differences include:

1. Building materials: some cultures build homes of wood, others of stone, and others of earth. People build homes with the materials available in their geographical regions.

2. Beauty: people build homes that look pleasing to them, homes that fit their idea of beauty. In Europe, new homes are often built to look like those that have stood in villages for hundreds of years. Among the Bedouin of North Africa, homes are not permanent structures, but brilliantly colored tents festooned with tassels and fringes.

3. Use: people build homes primarily for shelter but also to fit the way they live. A Masai cattle herder needs a place within his home, or **shamba**, to corral livestock. An Inuit needs shelter from the Arctic winds as well as access to fishing. An American suburbanite needs to be near transportation to the city. Homes are also designed to suit different climates and amounts of space. For example, many houses in cold climates are insulated between the inside and outside walls, floors, and ceilings. In tropical climates, walls made of a single layer of bamboo or reeds provide shelter from the hot sun.

Houses built along the rivers and rice paddies of Asia are often built on stilts to protect dwellers from rising and falling water levels.

Food! Glorious Food!

What people in a group eat is part of their culture. The food culture is created by tastes and influenced by religion and customs. A group's diet is also determined by what it can grow or raise. Climate, too, influences how people build their kitchens and prepare their foods.

Location determines dietary factors in many cultures. However, nowadays, because of excellent transportation and storage, canned goods are found in the homes of Arctic Inuits and frozen meals in the homes of people in desert regions.

Cuisine means a particular style of cooking or preparing food. Cuisine is determined by everything from taste to climate, farming, and location. For example, the cuisines of Asia use rice as a main ingredient. In Italian cuisine, wheat flour noodles called pasta are common. Cuisine is another way of saying "food culture." Today, with mass communication, migration, and transportation, many cuisines are available all over the world. Chinese and Italian cuisines, for example, are enjoyed by people in restaurants all over North America. Once an American phenomenon, fast foods, such as hamburgers and fries, are available in cities as far away as Beijing, China, and São Paulo, Brazil.

Political Systems

Political systems are **governments**, or the ruling bodies of the world's peoples. People who live under one government form a **country** or **nation**.

What Is Government?

A political system or *government* provides a set of laws and rules. There are many types of political systems, including:

Anarchy	No government or organized authority.
Confederacy	An alliance of separately governed states.
Democracy	A nation in which power rests with the people and is exercised directly by them or their elected representatives.
Dictatorship	A nation in which absolute power is controlled by a person whose position is not inherited.
Empire	A group of nations or territories ruled by one leader or country.
Monarchy	A nation ruled by a supreme sovereign, such as a king, queen, or emperor. In most monarchies, the rulers inherit their power. A constitutional monarchy is a system in which a king or queen is the head of state in a country ruled by a separate government.
Parliamentary Government	An assembly of persons, not necessarily elected, who write the laws of a nation or state.
Republic	A nation without a monarch and, in modern times, usually led by a president.

Chapter 4 How People Live

The Hunter-Gatherers

In ancient societies, people lived as **hunter-gatherers**. In some places today, they still do. That means they hunt, fish, and forage from the wild to find food.

Subsistence Farmers

To feed themselves, humans learned to sow plants and grow crops as well as to hunt and gather food. Over time, farmers learned to raise enough food to feed themselves.

Farmers who raise just enough food to feed themselves and their families are called **subsistence farmers**. Subsistence farming is still common in several parts of the world. In other parts, farming has become an industry or commercial activity (see below).

INDUSTRY & TECHNOLOGY

Industry means making products not simply for your use or your family's, but for sale to other people. Industries are divided into two categories: light and heavy.

Light industries	use lightweight raw materials to make clothes, food products, plants and flowers, furniture, and other consumer goods
Heavy industries	produce machines that do big jobs, such as cranes, oil derricks, cars, ships, airplanes, and farm equipment

There are many different types of light and heavy industries, but most fall into one of five categories:

1. **Agriculture**
2. **Mining**
3. **Forestry**
4. **Fishing and fishery**
5. **Manufacturing**

Technology is the use of scientific knowledge, usually to improve industry and commerce. Technology includes the machines and other tools used to work in a variety of industries, manufacturing (see p. 81), and arts and crafts (see p. 71).

Agriculture

Agriculture means farming. Farming began more than 10,000 years ago. Unlike hunter-gatherers who roamed from one place to another to find food, farmers built permanent homes and farmed the same land in the same area year after year.

Most of the food we eat and many of the materials for the things we use are grown on farms.

Some farms only grow plants, or crops, for food (fresh vegetables and fruits) or manufacture (wheat for flour, soybeans for meat substitutes, cotton for fabrics, corn for feed, etc.). Other farms use the land to graze animals. These are called livestock farms, and include farms where animals are raised to be processed into meat or to provide milk for dairy products (milk, cream, butter, cheese) and eggs. Some farms produce both crops and livestock. (These are called mixed farms.)

Old MacDonald Had a Farm

Old MacDonald had a farm—but just what kind of farm was it?

cooperative farm	Farm owned and operated by a group of farmers for the benefit of each individual involved.
corporate farm	Farm owned by a corporation, usually producing goods for sale in stores under a company label.
crop farm	Farm that raises food crops for harvest, such as vegetables, fruits, or grains.
dairy farm	Farm specializing in the production of milk, cheese, butter, and other dairy products.
family farm	Farm owned and operated by a family as a private business.
livestock farm	Farm specializing in raising animals, such as chickens, pigs, cows, goats, or buffalo, for egg, dairy, or meat production.
mixed farm	Farm where both livestock and crops are raised.
ranch	Farm specializing in one type of crop or livestock, such as a cattle ranch, mink ranch, or deer ranch.
subsistence farm	Farm on which food and other products necessary for life are grown by one family for its own use.
commercial farm	Farm specializing in products for sale to a wide market and intended to make profits from sales instead of products for family use.
plantation	Large farm or estate in a tropical or semitropical area, often specializing in commercial crops, such as cotton, tobacco, rice, sugar cane, coffee, or tea.
truck farm	Farm close to a city that specializes in vegetables, fruit, and other cash crops.
herding farm	Farm that uses large areas of land, usually arid, for herding goats, camels, sheep, and/or cattle.

World Agriculture

Estimated World Agricultural Workforce in 2000

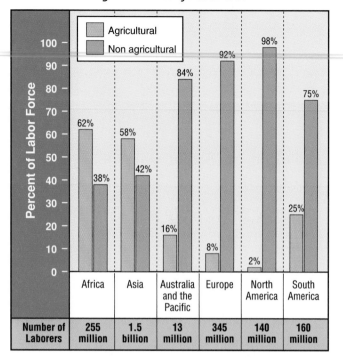

Number of Laborers	255 million	1.5 billion	13 million	345 million	140 million	160 million
	Africa	Asia	Australia and the Pacific	Europe	North America	South America

Estimated World Livestock Production by Region in 2000

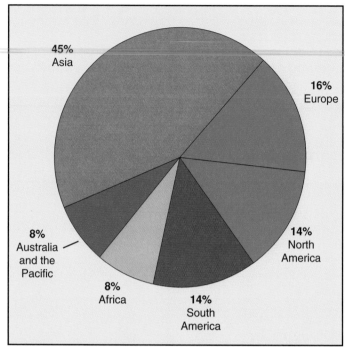

Both charts drawn from data collected from the Food and Agriculture Organization of the United Nations (2003) and *CIA World Factbook* (2003).

More than half the labor force—or almost two billion people—in Asia and Africa worked in agriculture in the year 2000, whereas only approximately 3 percent—or about 88 million people—worked in agriculture in the rest of the world. Yet these 88 million people produced almost half the world's crops. By comparing these graphs, you might conclude that most of the farming in Asia and Africa at the beginning of the twenty-first century was subsistence farming, not commercial farming.

Mining

Mining means taking rocks and minerals out of the earth. Many different rocks and minerals are mined, although they all fall into one of four categories:

Category	Example
metals	iron, lead, gold, silver, platinum
gemstones	diamonds, emeralds, rubies, sapphires, amethyst, lapis lazuli, jade
fossil fuels	natural gas, oil, coal
conglomerates	rock, sand, gravel

Some rocks and minerals are harder than others. The hardness is measured on the Mohs scale, a scale devised by the German scientist Friedrich Mohs. It ranks all rocks from 1 to 10.

MOHS SCALE

Softest	1	Talc
	2	Gypsum
	3	Calcite
	4	Fluorite
	5	Apatite
	6	Feldspar
	7	Quartz
	8	Topaz
	9	Corundum
Hardest	10	Diamond

Which Mine Is Mine? Different Types of Mining

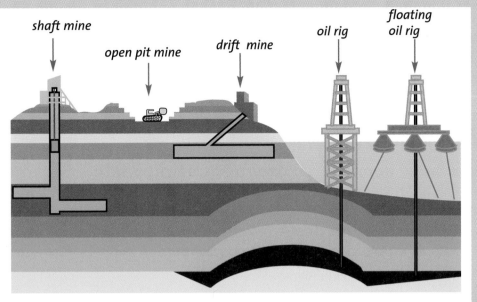

shaft mine

open pit mine

drift mine

oil rig

floating oil rig

Mining occurs above ground, deep underground, and even under the seas and oceans.

Some mineral resources are running low. If we continue to use minerals at our current rate, silver, gold, copper, natural gas, oil, iron ore, and uranium could be in short supply by 2050. However, because we recognize the danger, some people are using minerals more carefully. Also, geologists are searching for new deposits of these precious minerals on land and in the oceans.

Forestry

Forestry is the growing, maintaining, and harvesting of forests. Forests provide us with wood, which is used for building materials, furniture, paper, fuel, gums and resins, waxes, and medicines.

The world's forests come in many sizes and are filled with many different types of trees.

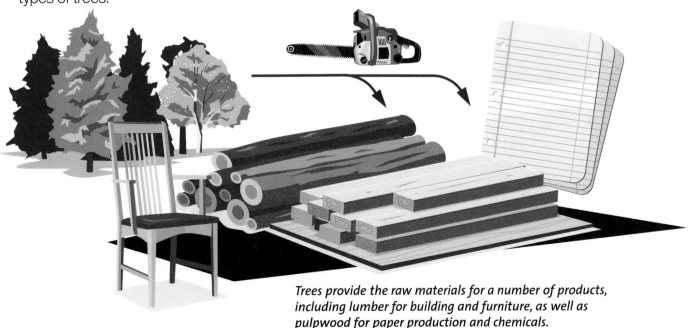

Trees provide the raw materials for a number of products, including lumber for building and furniture, as well as pulpwood for paper production and chemicals.

Fishing and Fisheries

The business of fishing is called *fishery*, and includes not only the catching and farming of fish and other aquatic animals, but also their processing and selling. Fishing is big business around the world. Nearly 80 million tons of sea animals are caught each year.

Manufacturing

Manufacturing means making new products from both raw materials and recycled materials. *Raw materials* are the natural products used to make new products. *Recycled materials* are the glass, metal, plastic, and paper collected from trash that are processed and reused to make new products.

1

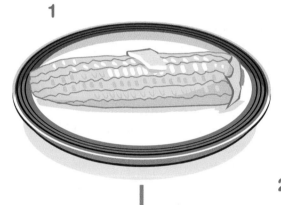

2

3

Corn is a versatile raw material. It is used as: 1. a food crop; 2. a raw material for producing corn oil and other processed foods and materials; and 3. a feed crop to support livestock.

A Brief History of Manufacturing

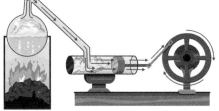

Machines such as the spinning wheel made cottage industries possible.

James Watt patented his steam engine in 1769, and the Industrial Revolution began.

The sewing machine made the creation of clothes easier for homemakers. It also made the garment industry possible because clothes could be mass-produced with the aid of this time-saving machine.

Before the 1700s, most people manufactured goods for their own use in their homes. People wove fleece and plant fibers into fabrics and made their own clothes. They caught fish and raised crops, and preserved and canned them. They cut trees to burn as fuel and to use as lumber to build houses, barns, fences, and more.

Later, people made things for other people from within their homes. For example, a tailor would sew not only for himself or herself, but also for those who paid for the service. A farmer might grow extra crops to sell at a farm stand, or a lumberer might fell logs for other people to build with or burn as firewood. People still manufacture products in their homes or in small local factories. These home-based manufacturing operations are called **cottage industries**.

In Europe, the early 1700s brought machines that made work easier and the production of manufactured products quicker and cheaper. The most important of these machines was improved and patented by the British inventor James Watt in 1769. It was the steam engine, and it brought about a change in the way people in Europe and the New World made products. This period of change is called the **Industrial Revolution**.

With the Industrial Revolution came many changes in the world of manufacturing and business. For example, instead of making one product at a time, the machines of the Industrial Revolution allowed for **mass production**, or the creation of many of the same products at the same time.

Many factory owners earned a great deal of money by selling mass-produced products. They built huge factories to make more and more products. To operate these factories, they hired many people. In fact, huge numbers of people moved into cities and factory towns during the Industrial Revolution to find work, live, and raise families.

Then, as today, businesses built or bought up other factories in different towns, cities, or even different states or countries. Companies with factories in two or more countries are called **multinational companies**.

Many items are produced on assembly lines, where different workers are responsible for separate tasks in the creation of a product. Cars are mass-produced, usually on assembly lines.

ARCTIC O

GREENLAND
(KALAALLIT NUNAAT)
(DENMARK)

Arctic Circle

NORWAY

DENMARK

ICELAND   NETHERLANDS

BELGIUM

UNITED
KINGDOM

FRANCE

IRELAND

LUXEMBOURG

SWITZERLAND

LIECHTENSTEIN

SLOVENIA

CROATIA

MONACO

ANDORRA

BOSNIA AND HERZEGOVINA

PORTUGAL

SPAIN

SAN
MARINO

VATICAN CITY

MONTENEGRO

KOSOVO

ALBANIA

MACEDONIA

MOROCCO

ALGERIA

ALASKA
(U.S.)

CANADA

ATLANTIC
OCEAN

UNITED STATES

30°N

MEXICO

BAHAMAS

CUBA

HAITI

Tropic of Cancer

JAMAICA

HAWAII
(U.S.)

BELIZE

GUATEMALA

EL SALVADOR

HONDURAS

NICARAGUA

COSTA RICA

PANAMA

PACIFIC
OCEAN

DOMINICAN
REPUBLIC

PUERTO RICO (U.S.)

VIRGIN ISLANDS (U.S., U.K.)

ST. KITTS AND NEVIS

ANTIGUA AND BARBUDA

DOMINICA

ST. LUCIA

ST. VINCENT
AND THE GRENADINES

BARBADOS

GRENADA

TRINIDAD AND TOBAGO

VENEZUELA

GUYANA

SURINAME

FRENCH
GUIANA
(FRANCE)

WESTERN
SAHARA
(MOROCCO)

CAPE VERDE

MAURITANIA

MALI

SENEGAL

BURKINA
FASO

GAMBIA

NIGER

GUINEA-BISSAU

GUINEA

SIERRA LEONE

LIBERIA

CÔTE d'IVOIRE

GHANA

TOGO

BENIN

SÃO TOMÉ
AND PRINCIPE

GABON

EQUATORIAL
GUINEA

REP.
OF THE
CONGO

ANGOLA

COLOMBIA

ECUADOR

Equator

0°

BRAZIL

PERU

TAHITI
(FRANCE)

BOLIVIA

PARAGUAY

Tropic of Capricorn

CHILE

30°S

URUGUAY

ARGENTINA

FALKLAND ISLANDS
(ISLAS MALVINAS)
(U.K.)

60°S

SOUTHERN
OCEAN

Antarctic Circle

ANTA

150°W   120°W   90°W   60°W   30°W   0°

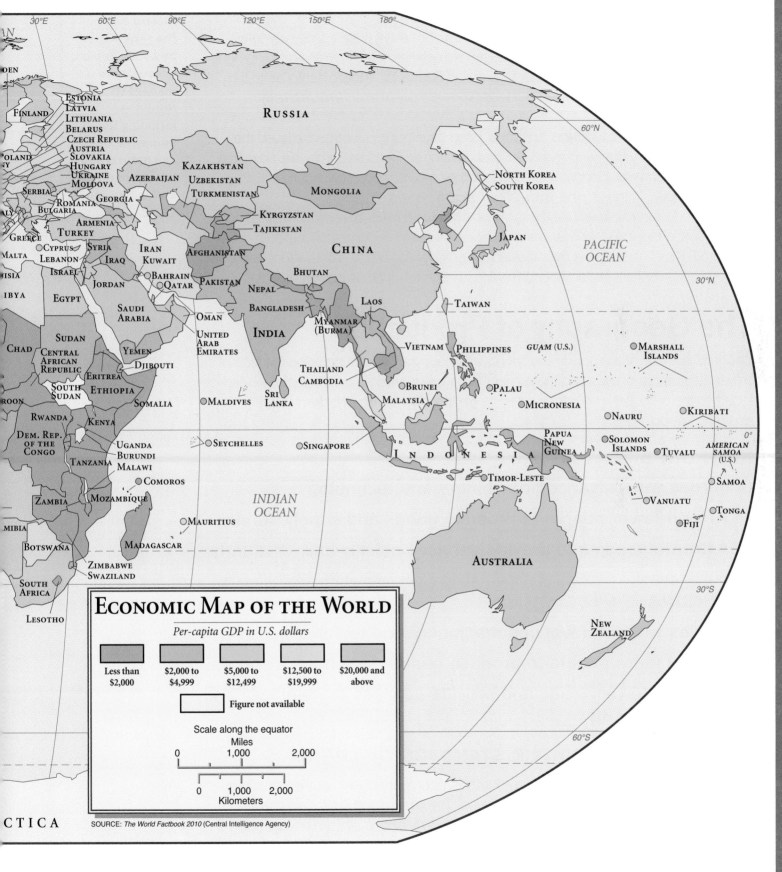

ECONOMIC MAP OF THE WORLD

Per-capita GDP in U.S. dollars

Less than $2,000	$2,000 to $4,999	$5,000 to $12,499	$12,500 to $19,999	$20,000 and above

Figure not available

Scale along the equator

Miles
0   1,000   2,000

Kilometers
0   1,000   2,000

SOURCE: *The World Factbook 2010* (Central Intelligence Agency)

Measuring Economies

Geographers study and compare the economies of different places. One way they measure an economy is by how much industry, sometimes called industrial development, a place has. Some countries, such as Taiwan and Russia, have lots of factories to turn natural resources into manufactured goods. They are considered *industrially developed*.

Other places, such as Mexico, are considered developing countries because they have some industry but need more. Still others, such as Chad or Cambodia, have little industrial development. Geographers consider their natural resources underused, or underdeveloped, in these *pre-industrial economies*.

Geographers sometimes use the term *postindustrial* to describe industrialized countries, such as the United States and Japan, that are no longer dominated by heavy industry. These postindustrial countries employ many workers to gather information, manage communications, and perform various services, such as banking or sales.

> An *economy* is the system used by a state, region, or country to manage its resources, including its money, labor, and natural and human-made materials.

The Geography of Production

Geographers look at the goods and services a country produces, including the tons of crops, the number of cars, and the number of people working in different jobs. Added together, the output of a country is called its *gross domestic product* (GDP). (See also map key pp. 82–83.)

HIGH GDPS

Countries with advanced machinery and technology:

1. Need fewer people to produce goods and supply services.

2. Create goods and provide services quickly and efficiently.

LOW GDPS

Countries without advanced machinery and technology:

1. Need more people to produce goods and supply services.

2. Create fewer goods and provide services more slowly and less efficiently.

DEVELOPMENT AND THE STANDARD OF LIVING

While GDP measures how productive a country is, geographers use another measurement when they look at how well individual people live. The *standard of living* shows how well the average person is able to find a job, a place to live, food, and an education. Generally, the more industrialized a country, the higher its standard of living. But this is not always true. For example, the standard of living in Kuwait, which has lots of oil but little other industry, is very high. On the other hand, one reason people in the former Soviet Union were dissatisfied is that they had a very low standard of living although their nation had a lot of industry.

Chapter 5

Migration, from Exploration to Settlement

An Overview of Migration

Scientists who study migration hypothesize that the first humans were born in Africa more than two million years ago and spread out from there into other parts of the world.

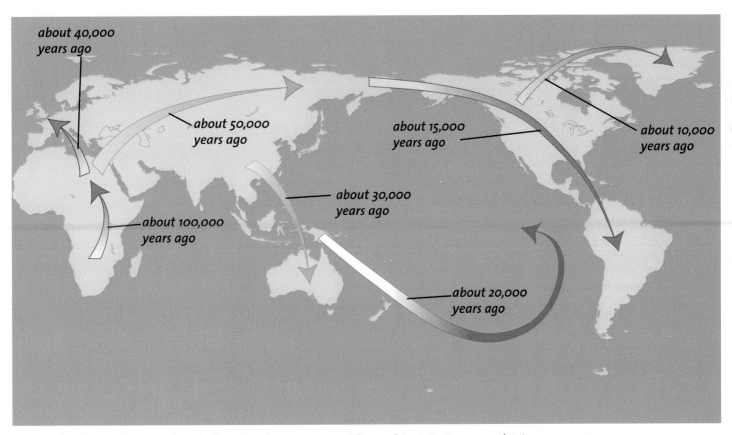

Many scientists and geographers believe that humans moved from Africa into Europe and Asia between 40,000 and 50,000 years ago. Then, over the next 30,000 years, they spread further to inhabit all the continents except Antarctica and many Pacific islands.

CONQUEST AND EMPIRE

In Europe in the late 1400s, an era called the **Age of Exploration** began. During this era, explorers made voyages to areas unknown to Europeans. Soon Europeans began to colonize and settle in many new places.

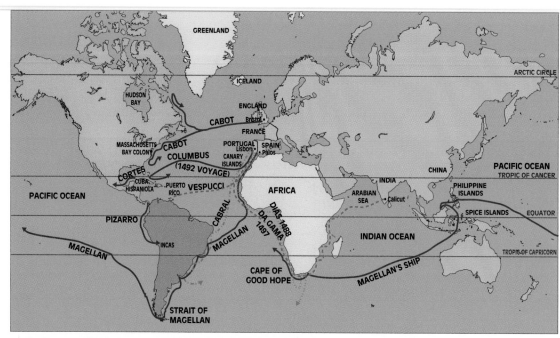

Routes of some major voyages led by European explorers.

Migration means movement from one place to settle in another. *Emigration* means movement away from one's homeland. *Immigration* means movement into a new country.

Can't Get There from Here: Transportation

In order for people to move from one region to another, they need **transportation** for themselves and their possessions. Early transportation was by foot. People simply walked from one place to another. Later, animals—horses, mules, and oxen—were tamed and used to carry passengers or packages, as well as to pull carts, sleds, and carriages.

With the Industrial Revolution (see p. 81) came the invention of machines to transport people farther in less time.

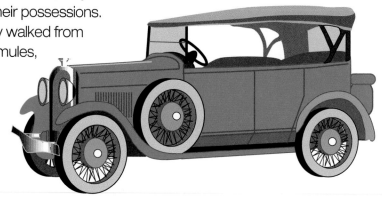

One of the products of the Industrial Revolution was the automobile.

Why Move?

People usually move from one place to another in search of a better place to live. Although there are many things that make one place better or worse than another, these things fall into two main categories:

1. Economics

2. Politics

PEOPLE MOVE AWAY FROM: **TO:**

Poverty	Areas of greater wealth	**ECONOMIC REASONS**
Overcrowded conditions	Greater space and comfort	
High cost of living	Affordable goods, services, and housing	
Lack of jobs	More work opportunities	**ECONOMIC AND POLITICAL REASONS**
Poor schools	Greater educational opportunities	
Poor health care	Available, higher-quality, health care	**POLITICAL REASONS**
Intolerance of race, culture, or religion	Tolerance	
Political oppression	Political choice and rights	
War or crime	Peaceful, safe life	

Glossary of Geographical Terms

Chapter **1**

acid rain	Rain that is polluted by acid in the atmosphere and damages the environment.
agriculture	Using the land to grow crops and raise animals; farming (see p. 77). (see p. 77)
Antarctic Circle	A line of latitude that lies 66 degrees 30 minutes (66° 30′) south of the equator. From September 21 to December 21, the area south of the Antarctic Circle has daylight more than 12 hours a day. On December 21, there is daylight for 24 hours at the Antarctic Circle, then, the days get shorter until there is darkness for 24 hours on June 21.
aquifer	A layer of rock that holds water in its pores.
archipelago	A group of small islands.
Arctic Circle	A line of latitude that lies 66 degrees 30 minutes (66° 30′) north of the equator. From September 21 to December 21, the area north of the Arctic Circle is increasingly in darkness. It has 24 hours of darkness on December 21 and then daylight begins at the Arctic Circle and moves north to the pole. On March 21, the area within the Arctic Circle has 12 hours of daylight and 12 hours of darkness. From March 21 on, the hours of daylight increase until the sun shines for 24 hours on June 21.
arid	Land that is arid is extremely dry because very little rain has fallen on it.
arroyo	A dry stream bed.
arts, fine	Visual, literary, and movement arts that communicate what a culture finds beautiful.

atoll	A horseshoe-shaped island formed by coral and surrounding a lagoon.
bank, river	The land along the sides of a river or canal.
basin, river	Land drained by a river or a river system.
bay	A curved area along a coast or shore where the water juts into the land. A bay is usually smaller than a gulf and usually has a smaller opening.
bayou	A system of swampland with slow-moving streams flowing through it, found in the southern United States.
bedrock	The solid rock that lies beneath the soil on the earth's surface.
beliefs	Attitudes, ideas, and world views held by a person or group of people.
birth rate	The number of babies born alive as a proportion of the population in a specific place in a specific amount of time.
blizzard	Heavy snowfall with high wind.
bog	A small, very acidic body of water that has no natural inlets and is surrounded by rings of vegetation. A mat of grasses may grow on top. As the grasses die and build up, the bog water is replaced by a spongy mass of peat.
branch	One of the two main streams that join to form a larger river.
butte	A flat-topped hill formed when hard rock on the surface protects softer soil underneath it from being eroded. A butte is often steep-sided.
canyon	A valley with very steep sides and a flat bottom, usually cut into the rock by a river. A canyon is larger than a gorge.
cape	A point of land that extends into a sea or an ocean.
chinook	A warm, dry wind that blows down the slopes of the Rocky Mountains in winter and in early spring, and melts the snow at the base of the mountains.
city	A place where a large number of people live close together; an urban area.
cliff	A high, steep rock face.
climate	The usual weather in a particular place over a period of time.
coast	The land beside a sea or ocean.
commercial area	A part of a city where business or industry is located.

continent	A large mass of land surrounded by oceans.
continental climate	A type of climate with hot summers and cold winters, common in the center of a continent.
continental divide	A highland or ridge of mountains that causes rivers and streams to flow in different directions across continents, eventually reaching different oceans.
continental drift	The movement of the continents on the earth's surface.
continental shelf	The part of the continents that extends below sea level toward the deeper ocean.
core	The center part of the earth, consisting of a molten outer core and a solid inner core.
course, river	The part of a river between its source and its mouth.
crater	The cup-shaped indentation at the top of a volcano.
crevasse	A deep crack in a glacier.
crust	The outer layer of the earth.
cuisine	A particular style of preparing food.
culture	The behavior—language, beliefs, traditions, arts and crafts, political systems, and technologies—of a group of people.
current	Cold and warm "rivers" of seawater that flow in the oceans. Also, streams of cold or warm air that flow through the atmosphere.
customs	The traditions of a group of people.
cyclone	A name for various air movements involving spiral motion, including typhoons, hurricanes, and tornados. Also the common name for a hurricane-type storm on the Indian Ocean.
delta	An area of land shaped like a triangle where a river deposits mud, sand, or pebbles as it enters the sea.
desert	A dry region, with fewer than 10 inches of precipitation annually.
developed country	A developed country has a lot of industry and a high standard of living.
developing country	A developing country has little industry and a low standard of living.
divide	High land—either a hill or a mountain—that causes rivers to flow in different directions.

downstream	The direction of a river's flow.
downtown	The main business area of a city.
drainage	The running off of rainwater from land.
drift	Soil, silt, and rock deposited by a glacier.
drought	An extra-long period without precipitation.
drumlin	A long, narrow hill formed by glacial deposits.
dune	A hill of sand formed by blowing winds.
eclipse, lunar	Event that occurs when light from the sun is blocked by the earth passing between the sun and moon, so that the earth casts a shadow on the moon (see p. 14).
eclipse, solar	Event that occurs when sunlight is blocked by the moon as it passes between the sun and earth, casting a shadow on the earth (see p. 14).
economy	The system used by a state, region, or country to manage its industry, trade, and finance.
equator	A line on a map or globe halfway between the north and south poles. The equator is almost 25,000 miles around.
escarpment	A cliff or steep bank located inland rather than at the shore.
esker	A long, narrow ridge of coarse gravel deposited by a stream flowing under or through a glacier.
estuary	The part of a river affected by the tides of the sea into which it flows.
exurb	A sparsely populated residential area just outside the suburbs of a city.
fall line	The region where elevation drops and rivers descend over a waterfall or rapids to lower elevations.
fault	A huge crack in the earth's surface, usually caused by movement of the earth's crust.
fishery	The business of fishing; also, a fish farm.
floodplain	The low, flat area on either side of a river that the river floods in times of high water.
forest	A large, dense growth of trees, plants, and underbrush.
forestry	The process of growing, maintaining, and harvesting forests.

fork	A separation into two or more branches, as of a stream.
geographic grid	The intersecting pattern formed by lines of longitude and latitude.
geographic north pole	Also *true north pole*. The point on the earth located at 90 degrees (90°) north latitude, where the lines of longitude meet.
geography	The study of the world, how it works, and how people use and change the world as they live in it.
geopolitical	A geopolitical map shows both political and physical features.
geyser	A spout of water heated by molten rock underground.
glacier	A thick bed of ice that covers a continent or a river of thick ice that moves slowly down a slope or valley.
globe	A sphere-shaped model of the earth.
gorge	A steep-sided, V-shaped canyon, usually caused by swiftly flowing water.
gross domestic product	The total output of a country or region, including all its products and the labor of its people. (GDP)
groundwater	Water found beneath the earth's surface.
gulf	A large area of sea that is partly surrounded by land.
headwater	The source of a river or river system.
hemispheres	Halves of the earth. The equator divides the earth into northern and southern hemispheres. The prime meridian and 180 degrees (180°) longitude divide the earth into eastern and western hemispheres.
hill	A part of the earth's surface that rises gently above the level of the surrounding land.
humid	When air is humid, it contains a lot of moisture.
humus	Soil made up of decomposed animals and plants.
hurricane	A violent, usually late-summer storm in the Atlantic Ocean.
iceberg	A mass of floating ice broken off from a glacier. Only a small patch of an iceberg shows above water.
ice-cap climate	An area with an ice-cap climate is constantly covered by snow and ice.
ice floe	A sheet of floating, frozen seawater.
industry	The making and selling of products.
inland waterway	Transportation pathway by means of navigable rivers, lakes, and streams in inland areas.

international date line	A line on a map or globe drawn from the north pole to the south pole, roughly following 180 degrees (180°) longitude, but turning and twisting to miss islands and other bodies of land. It is where the days of the week change. It is one day earlier east of the date line than it is west.
island	A body of land completely surrounded by water.
isthmus	A narrow strip of land that connects two larger bodies of land.
jungle	A very dense tangle of tropical vegetation.
lagoon	A shallow body of calm water separated from the sea by a narrow strip of land.
lake	A body of water surrounded by land. The water in lakes is usually fresh, but may be salty.
landform	Any of a number of natural features on the earth's surface, including mountains, plains, plateaus, hills, canyons, cliffs, etc.
language	The use of voice sounds, gestures, and written symbols to communicate thoughts and feelings.
leeward	Facing the direction toward which the wind is blowing.
loam	Soil that contains sand and clay as well as silt and humus.
loess	Fine soil particles and dust that are carried by the wind and water and pile up to form a rich, thick soil.
magnetic north pole	The point on the earth to which a magnetized compass needle points.
mantle	The part of Earth that lies between the core and the crust.
manufacturing	The creation of products from raw and recycled materials.
map	A picture of a place drawn on a flat surface.
marine climate	A mild and wet climate usually found near the sea.
marsh	A body of moving water, fresh or salty, with reeds growing in it. A marsh is usually near a river or sea coast.
megalopolis	A group of cities whose boundaries have extended to meet each other.
mental maps	Pictures in your mind of familiar places or regions.
mesa	A hill or mountain feature with a flat top and steep sides. A mesa is larger than a butte.
metropolis	A large city.
migration, human	The movement of people from one place to another, usually for economic or political reasons.

mining	Taking rocks and minerals out of the earth.
mistral	A strong, cold, dry northerly wind that sometimes brings very cold air down the Rhone River Valley in France.
monsoon	Seasonal reversal in wind direction that brings heavy rainfall in parts of southern Asia.
moraine	A mound of soil and pebbles carried by a glacier and dropped when the glacier receded.
mountain	A part of the land that rises abruptly to at least 1,000 feet above the surrounding land.
mouth, river	The place where a river flows into a larger body of water.
neighborhood	Area within a city or town that has a unique cultural makeup.
north pole	See **geographic north pole** and **magnetic north pole**.
oasis	A place in a desert where there is a source of water that can support some plant life.
ocean	A large body of saltwater that separates continents.
oxbow	A U-shaped bend in a river.
pampa	Large grassy plain of South America.
peak	The highest point of a mountain.
peninsula	A piece of land that juts into a body of water and is surrounded by water on three sides.
permafrost	Permanently frozen subsoil.
plain	Nearly flat region of land.
plate	One of the hard sections of the earth's crust on which the continents lie.
plateau	A large, mostly level area of land that stands higher than the surrounding area. A plateau is larger than a butte.
political system	Any type of government.
pond	A small body of fresh water.
population	The total number of people who live in a particular place.
population data	Facts about populations, including history, migration patterns, and cultural information.
population profile	A graph that shows different age groups within a population.
population pyramid	A bar graph that shows total population in terms of age and gender.

postindustrial economy	An economy that was once based on industry but is now based on services such as banking, computers, and health care.
prairie	Treeless plain, usually covered by tall grass.
precipitation	Any of the forms in which water falls on the earth's surface (rain, snow, hail, etc.).
pre-industrial economy	An economy with very little industry.
prevailing wind	The direction the wind usually blows across a particular place or region.
prime meridian	The line of longitude drawn from the north pole to the south pole at zero degrees (0°).
projections, map	Representations of the geographic grid used to make world maps.
rain forest	Forest in tropical climates with dense canopies, vines, and understories of growth.
range	A large area of open land. Animals usually graze on the grass on range lands.
range, mountain	A group or chain of mountains.
ravine	A deep, narrow canyon.
reef	A ridge of sand, coral, or bedrock under water but near the surface.
rift valley	A valley formed by the folding and the faulting of the earth's crust along parallel lines.
river	A large stream that flows from a source to a larger body of water, for example, a larger river, lake, sea, or ocean.
rural	A rural area is made up of farmland or countryside.
savanna	Tropical grassland with few trees.
sea	A large body of salt water surrounded partly by, or located next to land.
seamount	Underwater mountain with steep sides that rises from the ocean floor.
shore	The land beside a body of water.
silt	Fine grains of soil carried by water.
soil	Particles of bedrock, decomposed animal and plant matter, water, and air pockets that cover the earth's surface and that plants grow in.
source, river	The beginning of a river.

south pole	The point on the earth located at 90 degrees (90°) south latitude where the lines of longitude meet.
standard of living	A measurement of the availability of jobs, housing, food, and education to average citizens in a specific area or country. A high standard of living means greater availability; a low standard, lesser availability.
steppe	Any of the vast, treeless plains found in southeastern Europe and Asia.
steppe climate	Dry climate, but with greater precipitation than in a desert climate.
strait	A narrow body of water that connects two larger bodies of water.
stream	A small river.
suburb	Residential area lying just outside a city or town.
swamp	A wetland similar to a marsh but usually larger in area. It supports a wider variety of plant life, including trees and shrubs.
tableland	A plateau.
taiga	Cool, high-latitude land with low trees.
technology	The use of scientific knowledge, usually to improve industry or commerce.
tectonic plates	The pieces of the earth's crust that float on the mantle.
temperate climate	A climate without extremes of either heat or cold.
temperature	A measurement of heat.
thunderstorm	A storm accompanied by lightning, thunder, heavy rain, and sometimes hail.
tide	A change in the level of an ocean or a sea, both daily and over a year, due to the pull of gravity between the earth and the moon.
till	Soil and rock deposits spread out by a glacier as it moves or melts.
tornado	Violent and destructive cyclone that occurs inland.
trade wind	The prevailing wind of the tropics.
tributary	A stream or river that flows into a larger stream or river.
Tropic of Cancer	A line of latitude that runs parallel to the equator. It is located at 23 degrees 30 minutes (23° 30′) north of the equator. During the summer solstice (June 21), the sun is directly overhead at the Tropic of Cancer.

Tropic of Capricorn A line of latitude that runs parallel to the equator. It is located at 23 degrees 30 minutes (23° 30′) south of the equator. During the winter solstice (December 21), the sun is directly overhead at the Tropic of Capricorn.

tsunami A huge wave that may sometimes move through the water faster than 400 miles an hour and reach a height of more than 100 feet.

tundra A treeless plain in the Arctic where only mosses and low-growing plants can grow.

typhoon A violent late-summer storm in the northwest Pacific.

urban An urban area is a city or town.

valley A U-shaped lowland between hills or mountains.

volcano An opening in the earth's crust from which molten rocks erupt. The rocks usually form a mountain around the opening.

watershed Area whose rainfall runs, on the surface and as groundwater, to feed a particular river.

weather The conditions in the earth's atmosphere at a certain place and time.

weathering The breakdown of rock on the earth's surface due to wind, water, and chemical actions.

wind Air moving across the earth's surface.

windward Facing the direction from which the wind is blowing.

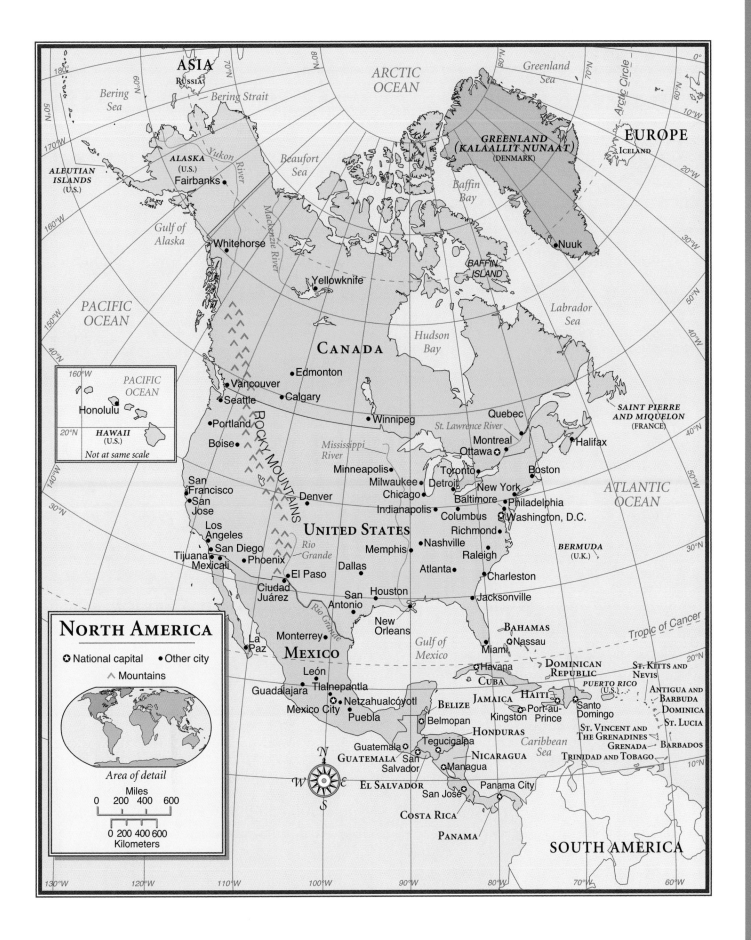

ASIA
Bering Sea
RUSSIA
Bering Strait
ARCTIC OCEAN
Greenland Sea
Arctic Circle
EUROPE

ALEUTIAN ISLANDS (U.S.)
ALASKA (U.S.)
Fairbanks •
Yukon River
Beaufort Sea
GREENLAND (KALAALLIT NUNAAT) (DENMARK)
ICELAND

Gulf of Alaska
Whitehorse •
Mackenzie River
Baffin Bay

PACIFIC OCEAN
Yellowknife •
BAFFIN ISLAND
Labrador Sea

CANADA
Hudson Bay

160°W
PACIFIC OCEAN
Honolulu
20°N
HAWAII (U.S.)
Not at same scale

• Edmonton
Vancouver •
• Calgary
Seattle •
Portland •
Boise •
ROCKY MOUNTAINS
• Winnipeg
Mississippi River
Quebec •
St. Lawrence River
Montreal •
Ottawa ✪
Halifax •

SAINT PIERRE AND MIQUELON (FRANCE)

San Francisco
San Jose
Denver •
Minneapolis •
Milwaukee •
Chicago •
Detroit •
Toronto •
Boston •
New York •
Baltimore •
Philadelphia •
ATLANTIC OCEAN

Los Angeles
San Diego •
Tijuana •
Mexicali •
Phoenix •
Rio Grande
UNITED STATES
Indianapolis •
Columbus •
Washington, D.C. ✪
Richmond •
Nashville •
Memphis •
Raleigh •
BERMUDA (U.K.)

El Paso •
Dallas •
Atlanta •
Charleston •
Ciudad Juárez
Rio Grande
San Antonio •
Houston •
Jacksonville •

La Paz •
Monterrey •
New Orleans
Gulf of Mexico
BAHAMAS
Nassau •
Tropic of Cancer

MEXICO
Miami •
Havana ✪
CUBA
DOMINICAN REPUBLIC
PUERTO RICO (U.S.)
ST. KITTS AND NEVIS

NORTH AMERICA

León •
Tlalnepantla •
Guadalajara •
Netzahualcóyotl •
Mexico City ✪
Puebla •
JAMAICA
HAITI
Kingston ✪
Port-au-Prince ✪
Santo Domingo ✪
ANTIGUA AND BARBUDA
DOMINICA
ST. LUCIA

✪ National capital   • Other city
⋀ Mountains

BELIZE
Belmopan ✪
HONDURAS
Tegucigalpa ✪
Caribbean Sea
ST. VINCENT AND THE GRENADINES
GRENADA
BARBADOS
TRINIDAD AND TOBAGO

Area of detail

Guatemala ✪
GUATEMALA
San Salvador ✪
EL SALVADOR
NICARAGUA
Managua ✪
San José ✪
Panama City ✪

Miles
0 200 400 600

COSTA RICA
PANAMA
SOUTH AMERICA

0 200 400 600
Kilometers

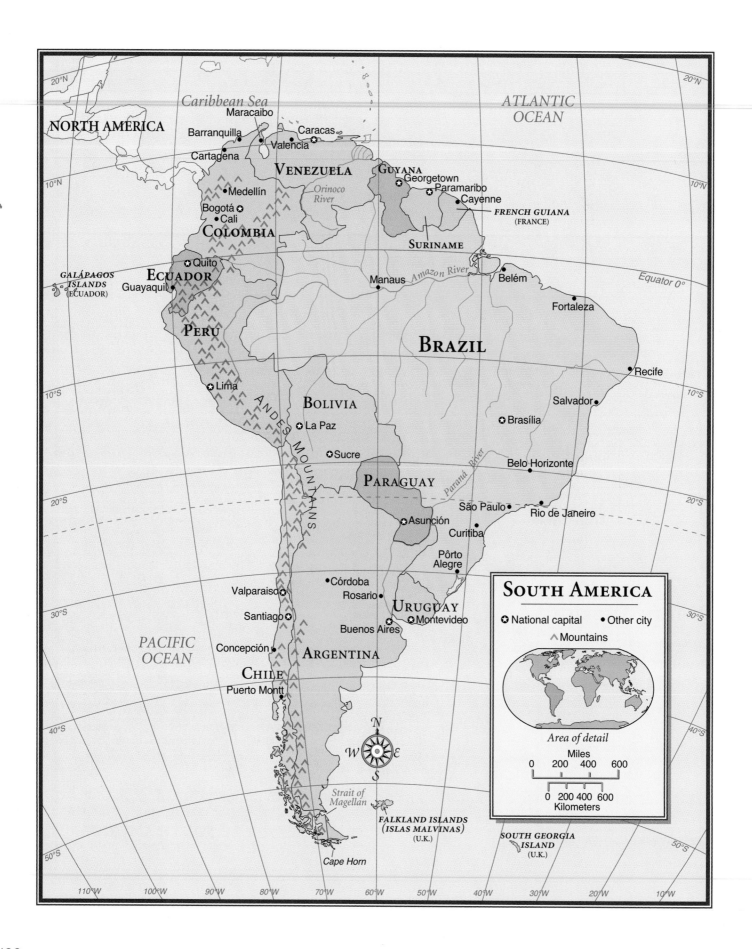

NORTH AMERICA

Caribbean Sea

ATLANTIC OCEAN

Maracaibo
Barranquilla
Caracas
Valencia
Cartagena

VENEZUELA

GUYANA
Georgetown
Paramaribo
Cayenne

Medellín

Orinoco River

FRENCH GUIANA
(FRANCE)

Bogotá
Cali

COLOMBIA

SURINAME

GALÁPAGOS ISLANDS
(ECUADOR)

Quito

ECUADOR

Guayaquil

Manaus

Amazon River

Belém

Equator 0°

Fortaleza

PERÚ

BRAZIL

Recife

Lima

ANDES MOUNTAINS

BOLIVIA

La Paz

Salvador

Brasília

Sucre

Belo Horizonte

PARAGUAY

Paraná River

São Paulo
Rio de Janeiro

Asunción

Curitiba

Pôrto Alegre

Córdoba
Rosario

Valparaíso

URUGUAY
Montevideo

Santiago

Buenos Aires

PACIFIC OCEAN

Concepción

ARGENTINA

CHILE

Puerto Montt

SOUTH AMERICA

⊛ National capital · Other city

⋀ Mountains

Area of detail

Miles
0 200 400 600

0 200 400 600
Kilometers

Strait of Magellan

**FALKLAND ISLANDS
(ISLAS MALVINAS)**
(U.K.)

**SOUTH GEORGIA
ISLAND**
(U.K.)

Cape Horn

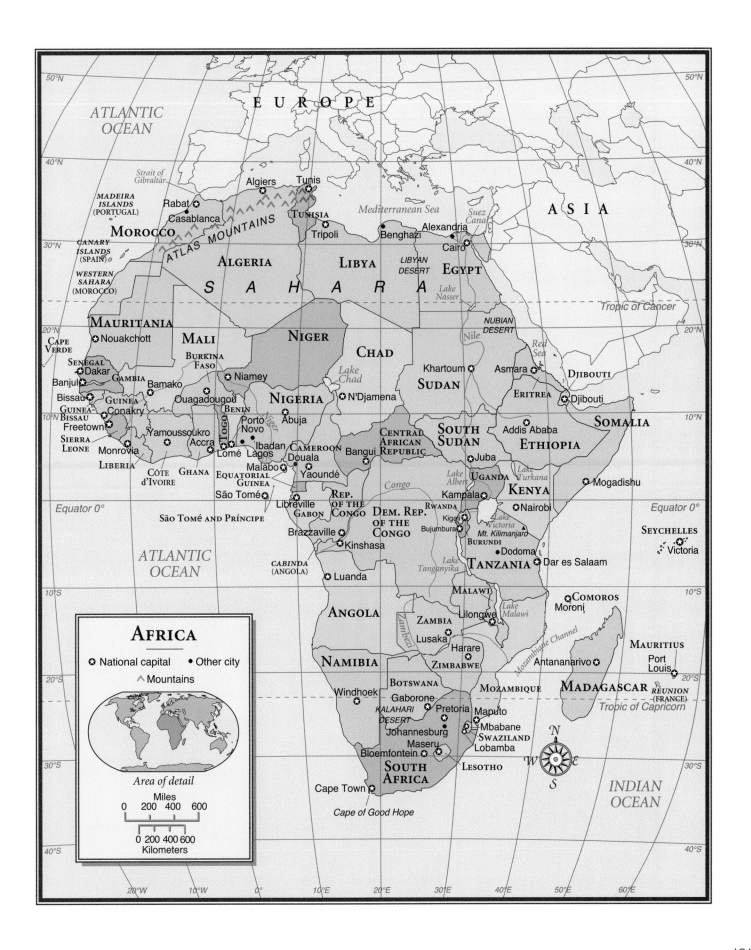

ATLANTIC OCEAN

EUROPE

Strait of Gibraltar

ASIA

Mediterranean Sea

Algiers
Tunis

MADEIRA ISLANDS (PORTUGAL)

Rabat
Casablanca
TUNISIA
Tripoli
Benghazi
Alexandria
Cairo
Suez Canal

MOROCCO

CANARY ISLANDS (SPAIN)

WESTERN SAHARA (MOROCCO)

ALGERIA
LIBYA
LIBYAN DESERT
EGYPT

S A H A R A
Lake Nasser

ATLAS MOUNTAINS

Tropic of Cancer

MAURITANIA
MALI
NIGER
CHAD
NUBIAN DESERT
Nile

CAPE VERDE

Nouakchott

BURKINA FASO

Khartoum
Asmara
DJIBOUTI

SENEGAL
Dakar
GAMBIA
Bamako
Niamey
Red Sea

Banjul
Bissau
Ouagadougou
N'Djamena
SUDAN
ERITREA
Djibouti

GUINEA-BISSAU
GUINEA
Conakry
NIGERIA
BENIN
Abuja
Niger

Freetown
SIERRA LEONE
Yamoussoukro
Accra
TOGO
Porto Novo
Ibadan
Lagos
CENTRAL AFRICAN REPUBLIC
SOUTH SUDAN
Addis Ababa
SOMALIA

Monrovia
Lomé
Malabo
CAMEROON
Douala
Bangui
Juba
ETHIOPIA

LIBERIA
CÔTE d'IVOIRE
GHANA
EQUATORIAL GUINEA
Yaoundé
Mogadishu

São Tomé
REP. OF THE CONGO
Lake Albert
UGANDA
Lake Turkana
KENYA

SÃO TOMÉ AND PRÍNCIPE
Libreville
GABON
Congo
Kampala
Nairobi

Brazzaville
DEM. REP. OF THE CONGO
Rwanda
Kigali
Lake Victoria
Equator 0°

Kinshasa
Bujumbura
BURUNDI
Mt. Kilimanjaro
Dodoma

CABINDA (ANGOLA)
Luanda
TANZANIA
Dar es Salaam

ATLANTIC OCEAN
Lake Tanganyika
SEYCHELLES
Victoria

MALAWI
COMOROS
Moroni

ANGOLA
ZAMBIA
Lilongwe
Lake Malawi

Lusaka
Harare

NAMIBIA
ZIMBABWE
Antananarivo
MAURITIUS
Port Louis

BOTSWANA
MOZAMBIQUE
MADAGASCAR
RÉUNION (FRANCE)

Windhoek
Gaborone
Tropic of Capricorn

KALAHARI DESERT
Pretoria
Maputo

Johannesburg
Mbabane
SWAZILAND
Lobamba

Maseru
Bloemfontein
LESOTHO

SOUTH AFRICA

Cape Town
N
W   E
S

Cape of Good Hope

INDIAN OCEAN

AFRICA

✪ National capital   • Other city

︿ Mountains

Area of detail

Miles
0 200 400 600

0 200 400 600
Kilometers

ARCTIC OCEAN

70°N

Norwegian Sea

FAEROE ISLANDS (DENMARK)

SHETLAND ISLANDS (U.K.)

SWEDEN

Gulf of Bothnia

FINLAND

NORWAY

Bergen

Oslo

Helsinki

Stockholm

Baltic Sea

Tallinn

ESTONIA

Göteborg

Riga

LATVIA

NORTHERN IRELAND (U.K.)

SCOTLAND

Edinburgh

North Sea

DENMARK

Copenhagen

LITHUANIA

RUSSIA

Vilnius

Belfast

Glasgow

ATLANTIC OCEAN

IRELAND

UNITED KINGDOM

Dublin

Manchester

NETHERLANDS

Hamburg

Elbe River

Berlin

Warsaw

POLAND

Lodz

Cork

Birmingham

WALES

ENGLAND

Amsterdam
The Hague

Rhine River

POLAND

Wroclaw

Krakow

London

Thames

BELGIUM

Brussels

Cologne

GERMANY

Vistula River

English Channel

Luxembourg

LUXEMBOURG

Prague

CZECH REPUBLIC

N
W   E
S

Paris

Seine River

LIECHTENSTEIN

Danube River

Vienna

Bratislava

SLOVAKIA

Loire River

Vaduz

Munich

AUSTRIA

Budapest

Nantes

FRANCE

Bern

SWITZERLAND

HUNGARY

Bay of Biscay

Bordeaux

Rhône River

Lyon

ALPS

Milan

Po River

SLOVENIA

Ljubljana

Zagreb

CROATIA

SERBIA

Toulouse

Turin

SAN MARINO

BOSNIA AND HERZEGOVINA

Belgrade

Porto

40°N

ANDORRA

Monaco

San Marino

Sarajevo

KOSOVO*

PORTUGAL

Andorra la Vella

Marseille

MONACO

VATICAN CITY

Adriatic Sea

MONTENEGRO

Pristina

Tagus River

Madrid

Barcelona

CORSICA (FRANCE)

Rome

Podgorica

Skopje

MACEDO

Lisbon

SPAIN

Tirana

ITALY

ALBANIA

Valencia

Naples

Seville

BALEARIC ISLANDS (SPAIN)

SARDINIA (ITALY)

Tyrrhenian Sea

GREEC

Strait of Gibraltar

GIBRALTAR (U.K.)

Mediterranean Sea

Palermo

Ionian Sea

SICILY (ITALY)

A F R I C A

Valletta MALTA

0°   10°E   20°E

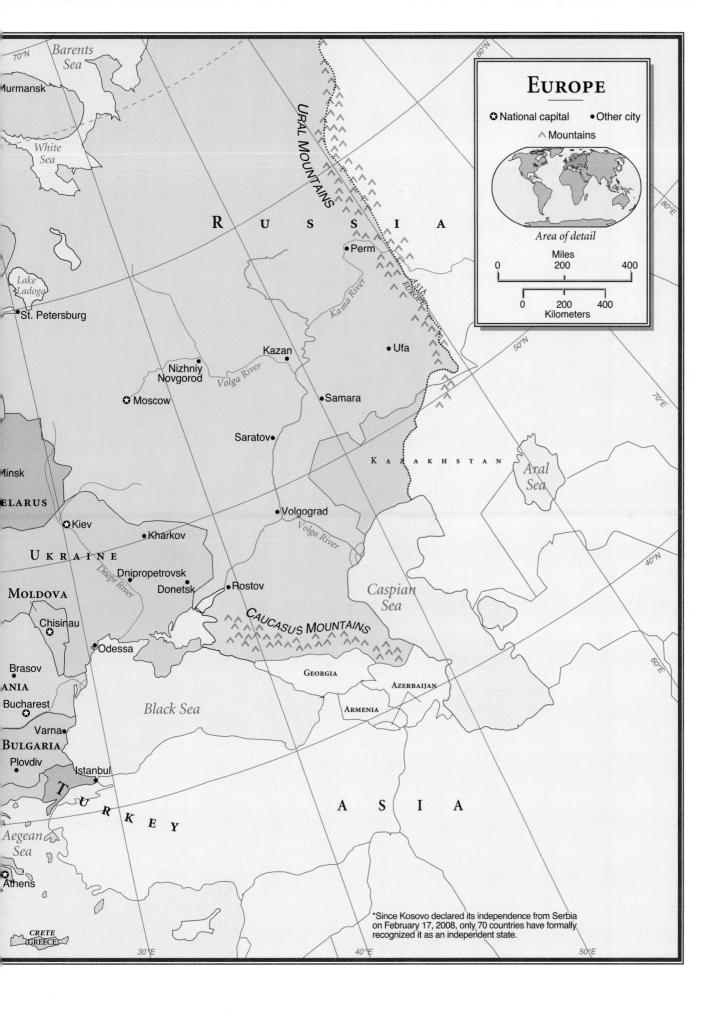

Barents
Sea

70°N

Murmansk

White
Sea

Lake
Ladoga

St. Petersburg

RUSSIA

URAL MOUNTAINS

60°N

• Perm

ASIA
EUROPE

Kama River

Kazan

Nizhniy
Novgorod

Volga River

• Ufa

☉ Moscow

• Samara

Saratov•

50°N

KAZAKHSTAN

Aral
Sea

Minsk

BELARUS

☉ Kiev

• Kharkov

• Volgograd

Volga River

UKRAINE

Dnipropetrovsk

Dnepr River

Donetsk

• Rostov

Caspian
Sea

MOLDOVA

Chisinau
☉

•Odessa

CAUCASUS MOUNTAINS

Brasov

ANIA

GEORGIA

AZERBAIJAN

Bucharest
☉

ARMENIA

Varna•

Black Sea

BULGARIA

Plovdiv
•

Istanbul

TURKEY

ASIA

Aegean
Sea

30°E

Athens
☉

40°E

50°E

CRETE
(GREECE)

40°N

70°E

60°E

EUROPE

☉ National capital   • Other city

⋀ Mountains

Area of detail

Miles
0   200   400

0   200   400
Kilometers

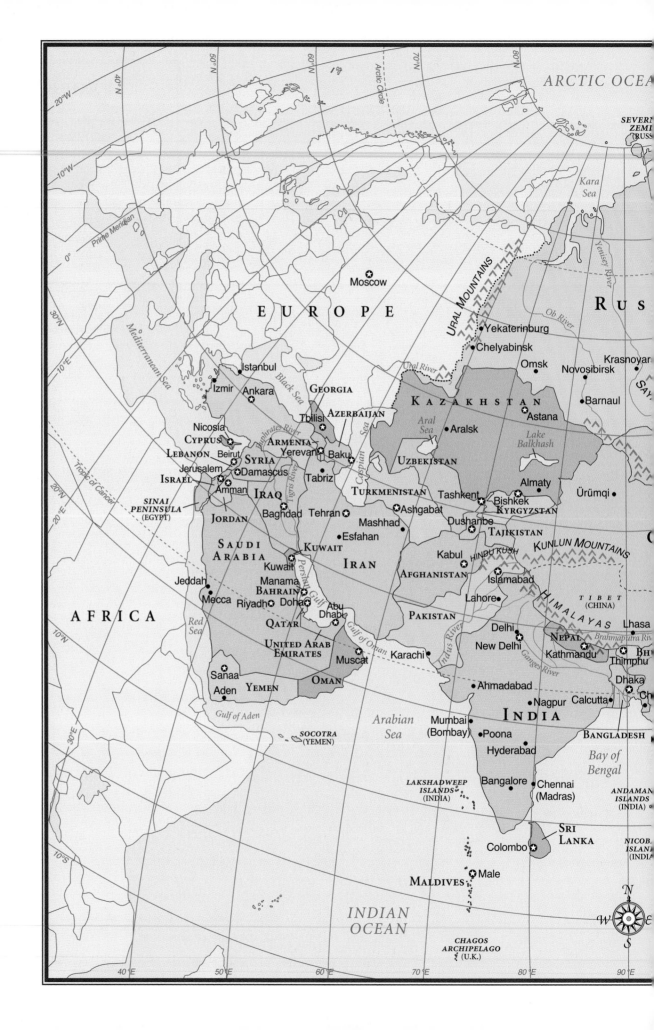

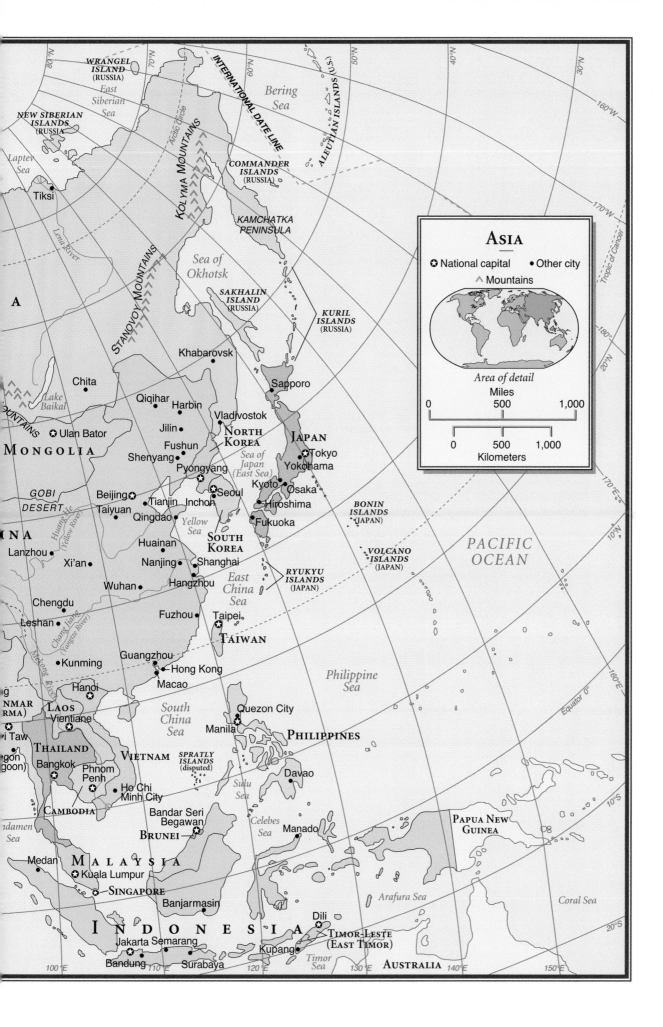

WRANGEL ISLAND (RUSSIA)

NEW SIBERIAN ISLANDS (RUSSIA)

East Siberian Sea

Laptev Sea

Tiksi

Lena River

KOLYMA MOUNTAINS

Arctic Circle

INTERNATIONAL DATE LINE

Bering Sea

ALEUTIAN ISLANDS (U.S.)

COMMANDER ISLANDS (RUSSIA)

KAMCHATKA PENINSULA

STANOVOY MOUNTAINS

Sea of Okhotsk

SAKHALIN ISLAND (RUSSIA)

KURIL ISLANDS (RUSSIA)

Khabarovsk

Chita

Lake Baikal

MOUNTAINS

A

MONGOLIA

Qiqihar

Harbin

Vladivostok

Sapporo

Jilin

NORTH KOREA

JAPAN

Fushun

Shenyang

Pyongyang

Tokyo

Sea of Japan (East Sea)

Yokohama

Ulan Bator

Kyoto

Osaka

GOBI DESERT

Beijing

Seoul

Hiroshima

Tianjin

Inchon

Taiyuan

Huang He (Yellow River)

Qingdao

Fukuoka

Yellow Sea

SOUTH KOREA

BONIN ISLANDS (JAPAN)

INA

Lanzhou

Huainan

Xi'an

Nanjing

Shanghai

VOLCANO ISLANDS (JAPAN)

PACIFIC OCEAN

Wuhan

Hangzhou

RYUKYU ISLANDS (JAPAN)

East China Sea

Chengdu

Chang Jiang (Yangtze River)

Leshan

Fuzhou

Taipei

Mekong River

TAIWAN

Kunming

Guangzhou

Hong Kong

Philippine Sea

Macao

Hanoi

Quezon City

NMAR RMA

LAOS

Vientiane

South China Sea

Manila

PHILIPPINES

i Taw

gon goon)

THAILAND

VIETNAM

SPRATLY ISLANDS (disputed)

Bangkok

Phnom Penh

Davao

Ho Chi Minh City

Sulu Sea

CAMBODIA

Bandar Seri Begawan

Celebes Sea

Manado

PAPUA NEW GUINEA

idamen Sea

BRUNEI

Medan

MALAYSIA

Kuala Lumpur

SINGAPORE

Arafura Sea

Coral Sea

Banjarmasin

Dili

INDONESIA

Jakarta Semarang

TIMOR-LESTE (EAST TIMOR)

Kupang

Timor Sea

AUSTRALIA

Bandung

Surabaya

ASIA

⊘ National capital   ● Other city

⌃ Mountains

Area of detail

Miles

0   500   1,000

0   500   1,000

Kilometers

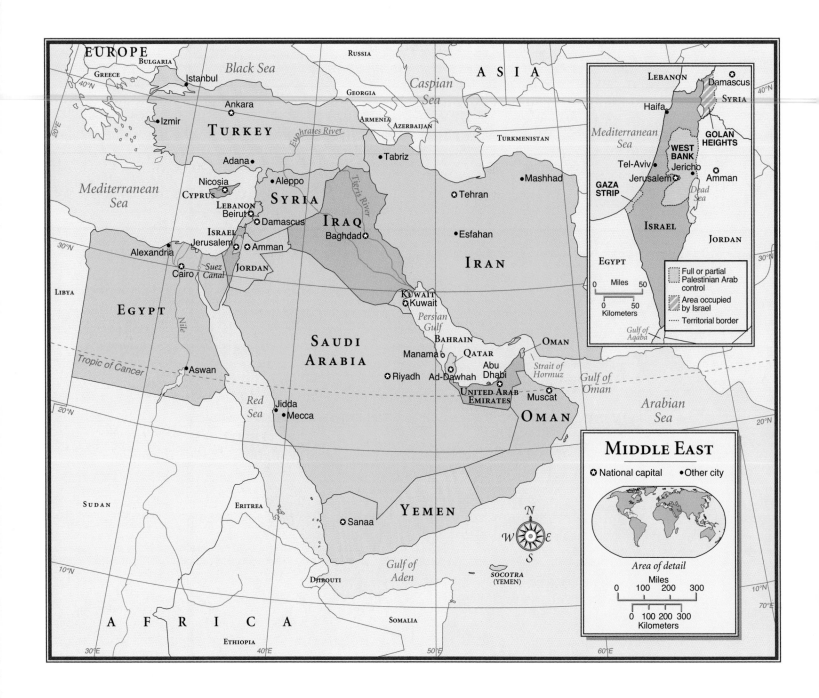

EUROPE

BULGARIA

GREECE

Izmir

Istanbul

Black Sea

RUSSIA

Caspian Sea

ASIA

40°N

20°E

Ankara

TURKEY

Adana

Euphrates River

GEORGIA

ARMENIA

AZERBAIJAN

TURKMENISTAN

40°N

Nicosia

CYPRUS

Aleppo

SYRIA

Tigris River

Tabriz

Mashhad

Mediterranean Sea

LEBANON

Beirut

Damascus

IRAQ

Tehran

ISRAEL

Jerusalem

Amman

Baghdad

Esfahan

IRAN

Alexandria

30°N

JORDAN

30°N

Cairo

Suez Canal

LIBYA

EGYPT

Nile

KUWAIT

Kuwait

Persian Gulf

SAUDI ARABIA

BAHRAIN

Manama

QATAR

OMAN

Tropic of Cancer

Aswan

Riyadh

Ad-Dawhah

Abu Dhabi

Strait of Hormuz

Gulf of Oman

UNITED ARAB EMIRATES

Muscat

20°N

Red Sea

Jidda

Mecca

OMAN

Arabian Sea

20°N

SUDAN

ERITREA

YEMEN

N

W E

S

SOCOTRA (YEMEN)

Sanaa

AFRICA

Gulf of Aden

DJIBOUTI

SOMALIA

ETHIOPIA

30°E

40°E

50°E

60°E

70°E

10°N

10°N

Inset map (upper right):

LEBANON

Damascus

SYRIA

Haifa

Mediterranean Sea

GOLAN HEIGHTS

40°N

WEST BANK

Tel-Aviv

Jericho

GAZA STRIP

Jerusalem

Amman

ISRAEL

Dead Sea

JORDAN

EGYPT

30°N

Miles

0   50

Kilometers

0   50

Gulf of Aqaba

Full or partial Palestinian Arab control

Area occupied by Israel

Territorial border

Inset map (lower right):

MIDDLE EAST

✪ National capital   • Other city

Area of detail

Miles

0   100 200   300

Kilometers

0 100 200 300

106

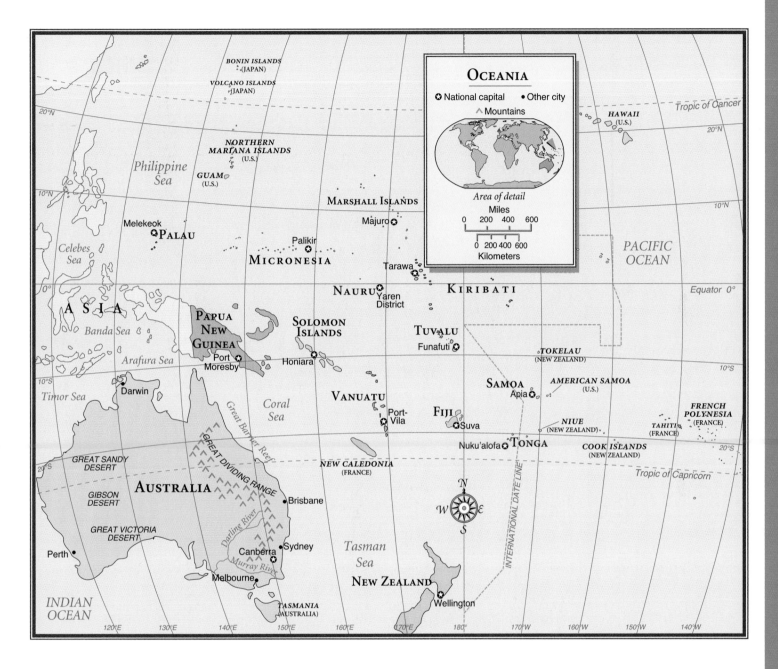

BONIN ISLANDS
(JAPAN)

VOLCANO ISLANDS
(JAPAN)

Tropic of Cancer

20°N   20°N

HAWAII
(U.S.)

Philippine
Sea

10°N   10°N

NORTHERN
MARIANA ISLANDS
(U.S.)

GUAM
(U.S.)

MARSHALL ISLANDS

Majuro ✪

PACIFIC
OCEAN

Celebes
Sea

Melekeok
✪ PALAU

Palikir
MICRONESIA

Tarawa ✪

OCEANIA

✪ National capital   • Other city

⋀ Mountains

Area of detail

Miles
0   200   400   600

Kilometers
0 200 400 600

ASIA

Banda Sea

NAURU ✪
Yaren
District

KIRIBATI

Equator 0°

PAPUA
NEW
GUINEA

SOLOMON
ISLANDS

TUVALU

Funafuti ✪

TOKELAU
(NEW ZEALAND)

10°S

Arafura Sea

Port
Moresby ✪

Honiara ✪

SAMOA
Apia ✪

AMERICAN SAMOA
(U.S.)

Darwin

Timor Sea

VANUATU

FIJI
Suva ✪

NIUE
(NEW ZEALAND)

FRENCH
POLYNESIA
(FRANCE)

Coral
Sea

Port-
Vila ✪

TAHITI
(FRANCE)

Nuku'alofa ✪ TONGA

COOK ISLANDS
(NEW ZEALAND)

20°S

GREAT SANDY
DESERT

GREAT DIVIDING RANGE

NEW CALEDONIA
(FRANCE)

Tropic of Capricorn

20°S

GIBSON
DESERT

AUSTRALIA

Brisbane

GREAT VICTORIA
DESERT

Perth

Canberra ✪ Sydney

Melbourne

Tasman
Sea

NEW ZEALAND

INDIAN
OCEAN

TASMANIA
(AUSTRALIA)

Wellington ✪

120°E   130°E   140°E   150°E   160°E   170°E   180°   170°W   160°W   150°W   140°W

Great Barrier Reef

Darling River

Murray River

INTERNATIONAL DATE LINE

N
W   E
S

PACIFIC OCEAN

BRITISH COLUMBIA
ALBERTA
SASKATCHEWAN
MANITOBA

VANCOUVER ISLAND
Vancouver
•Victoria
OLYMPIC N.P.
NORTH CASCADES N.P.
•Seattle
•Tacoma
★Olympia
MT. RAINIER▲ WASHINGTON
MT. RAINIER N.P.
•Spokane
•Portland
MT. ST. HELENS▲
★Salem
Columbia River
•Eugene
OREGON
CRATER LAKE N.P.
Medford•
REDWOOD N.P.
LASSEN VOLCANIC N.P.

Snake River
★Boise
IDAHO
Idaho Falls•
Pocatello○

GLACIER N.P.
•Great Falls
Missouri River
Butte•
MONTANA
•Helena
Billings•
Yellowstone River

YELLOWSTONE N.P.
GRAND TETON N.P.
WYOMING

•Calgary
★Regina
•Winnipeg

THEODORE ROOSEVELT N.P.
•Bismarck★ NORTH DAKOTA
Grand Forks
•Fargo
International Falls
Dulu
MINNESOTA
Aberdeen•
SOUTH DAKOTA
Rapid City•
★Pierre
BADLANDS N.P.
WIND CAVE N.P.
Minneapolis
St. Paul
Rochester
Sioux Falls•
Sioux City•

CAN

CAN
N

NEVADA
•Reno
•Carson City
Sacramento★
Stockton•
San Francisco•○ Oakland•
San José•
Fresno•
KINGS CANYON N.P.
SEQUOIA N.P. •MT. WHITNEY
CALIFORNIA
YOSEMITE N.P.
GREAT BASIN N.P.
Great Salt Lake
•Ogden
★Salt Lake City
Provo•
UTAH
CAPITOL REEF N.P.
BRYCE CANYON N.P.
ARCHES N.P.
CANYONLANDS N.P.

Laramie•
•Cheyenne★
North Platte•
ROCKY MOUNTAIN N.P.
BLACK CANYON OF THE GUNNISON N.P.
•Boulder
★Denver
•Aurora
•Colorado Springs
Pueblo•
COLORADO
MESA VERDE N.P.
GREAT SAND DUNES N.P.

NEBRASKA
Grand Island•
Lincoln•
IOWA
Des Moin
Omaha•
Topeka★
Kansas City
KANSAS
Arkansas River
•Dodge City •Wichita
MISSO
Kansas City
Indepe
Jeff

DEATH VALLEY N.P.
Las Vegas•
ZION N.P.
JOSHUA TREE N.P.
Los Angeles•
Long Beach•
•Anaheim
Santa Ana•
CHANNEL ISLANDS N.P.
Salton Sea
Colorado River
GRAND CANYON N.P.
ARIZONA
PETRIFIED FOREST N.P.
Phoenix•
•Mesa
San Diego•
•Tijuana
Gila River
SAGUARO N.P.
Tucson•

Santa Fe★
•Albuquerque
NEW MEXICO
•Amarillo
Lubbock•
CARLSBAD CAVERNS N.P.
OKLAHOMA
★Oklahoma City
Tulsa•
AR
Fort Smi
HOT SPRI

BAJA CALIFORNIA NORTE
SONORA
Juárez•
•El Paso
GUADALUPE MOUNTAINS N.P.
Rio Grande
Pecos River
TEXAS
Ft. Worth•
•Garland
•Dallas
Arlington•
Waco•
Brazos River
Colorado River
Shre
LO

CHIHUAHUA
MEXICO
COAHUILA
BIG BEND N.P.
San Antonio•
Austin★
Beaumont•
Houston•
•Galveston
•Laredo
Corpus Christi•
NUEVO LEÓN
•Matamoros
TAMAULIPAS

170°W 160°W 150°W 140°W 130°W 120°W
70°N
Barrow•
GATES OF THE ARCTIC N.P.
KOBUK VALLEY N.P.
ALASKA
Fairbanks•
Nome•
DENALI N.P.
MT. MCKINLEY▲
Anchorage•
LAKE CLARK N.P.
KENAI FJORDS N.P.
KATMAI N.P.
60°N
ALEUTIAN ISLANDS
KODIAK ISLAND
CANADA
WRANGELL– ST. ELIAS N.P.
Juneau•
GLACIER BAY N.P.
0   300 Miles
0   300 Kilometers

NIIHAU KAUAI
PACIFIC OCEAN
OAHU
Honolulu★ •MOLOKAI
LANAI MAUI
HALEAKALA N.P.
KAHOOLAWE
20°N
HAWAII
•Hilo
•HAWAII
0   100 Miles
0   100 Kilometers
160°W
HAWAII VOLCANOES N.P.

108

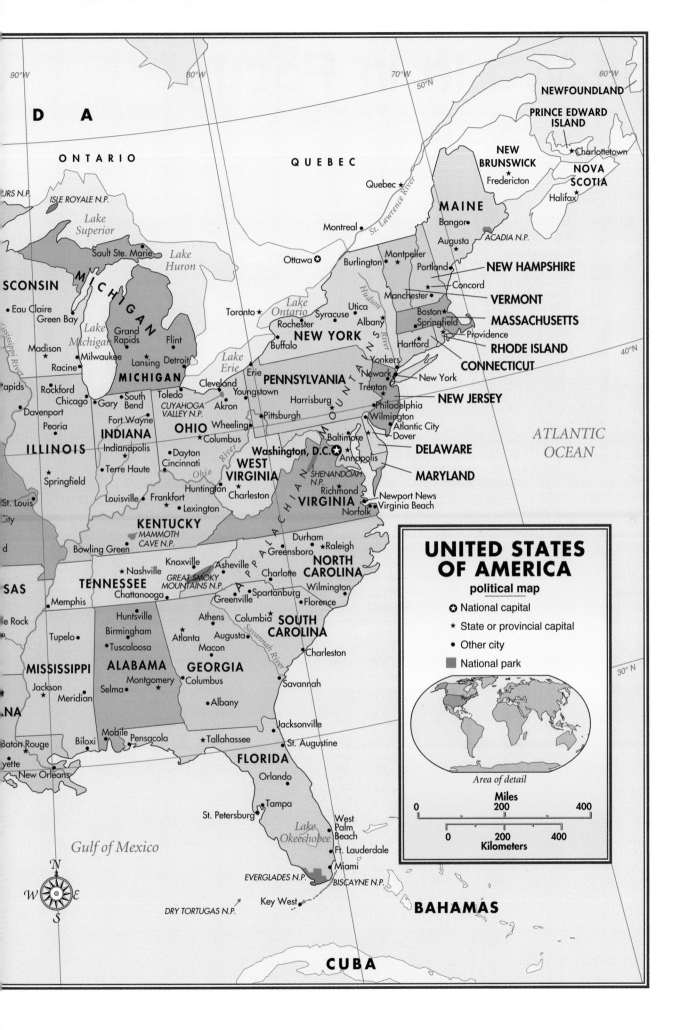

URS N.P.

ISLE ROYALE N.P.

ONTARIO

QUEBEC

Lake Superior

Sault Ste. Marie

Lake Huron

Ottawa ⊙

Quebec ★

Montreal

St. Lawrence River

NEWFOUNDLAND

PRINCE EDWARD ISLAND

NEW BRUNSWICK
Fredericton ★

★ Charlottetown

NOVA SCOTIA

Halifax

MAINE
Bangor
Augusta ★

ACADIA N.P.

SCONSIN

• Eau Claire
• Green Bay

Madison •
• Milwaukee
Racine •

Lake Michigan

MICHIGAN

Grand Rapids
Flint
Lansing • Detroit

MICHIGAN

apids

• Rockford
Chicago •
• Gary

Davenport •
Peoria •

ILLINOIS

• Springfield

St. Louis

City

d

Mississippi River

Burlington

Toronto ★

Lake Ontario

Rochester

Syracuse

Utica

Albany ★

Montpelier ★

Manchester •

Portland •

NEW HAMPSHIRE

★ Concord

VERMONT

Boston ★
Springfield •

MASSACHUSETTS

Providence ★

RHODE ISLAND

Hartford ★

CONNECTICUT

NEW YORK

Buffalo •

Erie

Lake Erie

Cleveland •

South Bend

Youngstown

Akron •

OHIO

Columbus ★

Fort Wayne

INDIANA

Indianapolis ★

• Dayton
Cincinnati •

• Terre Haute

CUYAHOGA VALLEY N.P.

Wheeling •

Pittsburgh •

PENNSYLVANIA

Harrisburg ★

Ohio River

WEST VIRGINIA

Huntington •

Charleston ★

APPALACHIAN MOUNTAINS

Hudson River

Yonkers
Newark ★
Trenton ★

New York

NEW JERSEY

Philadelphia •
Wilmington •
Atlantic City •
Dover ★

Baltimore •

Washington, D.C. ⊛

Annapolis ★

DELAWARE

MARYLAND

SHENANDOAH N.P.

ATLANTIC OCEAN

KENTUCKY

Louisville •
Frankfort ★
Lexington •

MAMMOTH CAVE N.P.

Bowling Green •

Richmond ★

VIRGINIA

Newport News
Virginia Beach

Norfolk •

SAS

• Memphis

Tupelo •

• Nashville

Knoxville •

Chattanooga •

TENNESSEE

GREAT SMOKY MOUNTAINS N.P.

Asheville •

Durham •
★ Raleigh
Greensboro •

NORTH CAROLINA

Charlotte •

Wilmington •

Spartanburg •
Greenville •
Florence •

le Rock

NA

Huntsville •
Birmingham •
• Tuscaloosa

MISSISSIPPI

Jackson ★
• Meridian

Athens •

Atlanta ★
Macon •

Columbia ★

SOUTH CAROLINA

Charleston •

Savannah River

Augusta •

ALABAMA

Montgomery ★
Selma •

GEORGIA

Columbus •

• Albany

Savannah •

Baton Rouge

yette

New Orleans

Biloxi •
Mobile •
Pensacola •

★ Tallahassee

Jacksonville •

★ Jacksonville

St. Augustine •

FLORIDA

Orlando •

Tampa •
St. Petersburg •

Lake Okeechobee

West Palm Beach

Ft. Lauderdale •
Miami •

EVERGLADES N.P.

BISCAYNE N.P.

Gulf of Mexico

DRY TORTUGAS N.P.

Key West •

BAHAMAS

CUBA

N
W E
S

UNITED STATES OF AMERICA
political map

⊛ National capital

★ State or provincial capital

• Other city

■ National park

Area of detail

Miles		
0	200	400

Kilometers		
0	200	400

90°W 80°W 70°W 50°N 60°W

40°N

30°N

Chapter 3

The World in Focus

Area & Population: Taken together, these figures allow you to calculate population density (population divided by area)—the average number of people who live on each square mile of land.

Urban Population: The percent of a country's total population living in urban areas.

Political System & Head of Government: Presidential-parliamentary systems split authority between a president (head of state) and a prime minister (head of government). The more powerful of the two is listed.

Date of Origin: The year in which a country declared independence, won control of its affairs, or established its present boundaries.
Literacy Rate: The percent of people who can read and write (male/female[1]).

Per Capita GDP: The value in U.S. dollars of all goods and services produced within a country in one year (its gross domestic product), divided by its population. It is one way to gauge a nation's wealth.

COUNTRY	AREA (SQ MI)	URBAN POP. %	CAPITAL	LANGUAGES	POLITICAL SYSTEM & HEAD OF GOVERNMENT	DATE OF ORIGIN	LITERACY RATE (%)	PER CAPITA GDP
	POPULATION	POP. RISE %/YEAR				% OF POP. UNDER 15	LIFE EXPECTANCY	HDI
France	212,934	77	Paris	French, regional dialects	Presidential-parliamentary democracy; President Nicolas Sarkozy	486	99/99	$32,600
	63,000,000	0.4				18	78/85	0.961

Percent of Population Increase: The birth rate minus the death rate of a country. Population growth in poor countries tends to be higher than in wealthier ones.

Languages Spoken: We show only major languages. Some 7,000 languages are spoken in the world, not counting local dialects. About 12 percent of all people speak Mandarin Chinese—more than double any other language.

Percent of Population Under Age 15: Developing countries with a high percentage of young people may have trouble providing enough jobs, schools, and food.

Life Expectancy: The age to which a newborn can expect to live. The first number is for males, the second for females.

HDI (Human Development Index): This number measures economic and human well-being on a scale of 0 to 1. It combines life expectancy, literacy, and purchasing power into one figure.

[1]When breakdown by gender is not available, a single figure represents the population as a whole.

COUNTRY	AREA (SQ MI) / POPULATION	URBAN POP. % / POP. RISE %/YEAR	CAPITAL	LANGUAGES	POLITICAL SYSTEM & HEAD OF GOVERNMENT	DATE OF ORIGIN / % OF POP. UNDER 15	LITERACY RATE (%) / LIFE EXPECTANCY	PER CAPITA GDP / HDI
Antigua and Barbuda	170 / 100,000	31 / 0.9	St. John's	English, English patois (PAH-twah)	Parliamentary democracy; Prime Minister Baldwin Spencer	1981 / 28	86 / 73/77	$17,800 / 0.868
Bahamas	5,359 / 300,000	83 / 0.9	Nassau	English, Creole	Parliamentary democracy; Prime Minister Hubert Ingraham	1973 / 26	95/97 / 71/77	$29,700 / 0.856
Barbados	166 / 300,000	38 / 0.5	Bridgetown	English, Bajan	Parliamentary democracy; Prime Minister David Thompson	1966 / 19	99/99 / 71/76	$17,700 / 0.903
Belize	8,865 / 300,000	51 / 2.3	Belmopan	English, Spanish, Mayan, Garifuna	Parliamentary democracy; Prime Minister Dean Barrow	1981 / 37	77/77 / 71/74	$8,300 / 0.772
Canada	3,849,670 / 34,100,000	80 / 0.4	Ottawa	English, French	Parliamentary democracy; Prime Minister Stephen Harper	1867 / 17	99/99 / 78/83	$38,200 / 0.966
Costa Rica	19,730 / 4,600,000	59 / 1.3	San José	Spanish, English	Presidential-legislative democracy; President Laura Chinchilla	1821 / 23	95/95 / 77/82	$10,900 / 0.854
Cuba	42,803 / 11,200,000	75 / 0.3	Havana	Spanish	Communist one-party state; President Raúl Castro	1902 / 18	99/99 / 76/80	$9,700 / 0.863
Dominica	290 / 100,000	73 / 0.7	Roseau	English, French patois	Parliamentary democracy; Prime Minister Roosevelt Skerrit	1978 / 23	94/94 / 72/78	$10,200 / 0.814
Dominican Republic	18,815 / 9,900,000	67 / 1.7	Santo Domingo	Spanish	Presidential-legislative democracy; President Leonel Fernández	1844 / 32	87/87 / 69/75	$8,300 / 0.777
El Salvador	8,124 / 6,200,000	63 / 1.4	San Salvador	Spanish, Nahua	Presidential-legislative democracy; President Mauricio Funes	1821 / 33	83/80 / 67/76	$7,200 / 0.747
Grenada	131 / 100,000	31 / 0.8	St. George's	English, French patois	Parliamentary democracy; Prime Minister Tillman Thomas	1974 / 31	96 / 68/72	$10,300 / 0.813
Guatemala	42,042 / 14,400,000	47 / 2.8	Guatemala City	Spanish, Amerindian dialects	Presidential-legislative democracy; President Álvaro Colom Caballeros	1821 / 42	75/63 / 66/73	$5,100 / 0.704
Haiti	10,714 / 9,800,000	48 / 1.8	Port-au-Prince	French, Creole	Presidential-legislative democracy (transitional); President René Préval	1804 / 37	55/51 / 59/62	$1,300 / 0.532
Honduras	43,278 / 7,600,000	50 / 2.3	Tegucigalpa	Spanish, Amerindian dialects	Presidential-parliamentary democracy in transition after coup; President Porfirio Lobo	1821 / 38	80/80 / 70/75	$4,100 / 0.732
Jamaica	4,243 / 2,700,000	52 / 1.2	Kingston	English, English patois	Parliamentary democracy; Prime Minister Bruce Golding	1962 / 28	84/92 / 68/75	$8,400 / 0.766
Mexico	756,062 / 110,600,000	77 / 1.4	Mexico City	Spanish, Mayan, other indigenous languages	Presidential-legislative democracy; President Felipe Calderón	1810 / 29	87/85 / 74/79	$13,200 / 0.854
Nicaragua	50,193 / 6,000,000	56 / 1.8	Managua	Spanish, English, Amerindian dialects	Presidential-legislative democracy; President Daniel Ortega	1821 / 35	67/68 / 69/73	$2,800 / 0.699
Panama	29,158 / 3,500,000	64 / 1.6	Panama City	Spanish, English	Presidential-legislative democracy; President Ricardo Martinelli	1903 / 30	93/91 / 73/78	$12,100 / 0.840
Saint Kitts and Nevis	139 / 100,000	32 / 0.7	Basseterre	English, English patois	Parliamentary democracy; Prime Minister Denzil Douglas	1983 / 24	98 / 71/76	$14,700 / 0.838
Saint Lucia	239 / 200,000	28 / 0.7	Castries	English, French patois	Parliamentary democracy; Prime Minister Stephenson King	1979 / 25	90/91 / 71/76	$10,900 / 0.821
Saint Vincent and the Grenadines	151 / 100,000	40 / 0.9	Kingstown	English, English patois	Parliamentary democracy; Prime Minister Ralph Gonsalves	1979 / 28	96/96 / 70/74	$10,200 / 0.772
Trinidad and Tobago	1,981 / 1,300,000	12 / 0.6	Port-of-Spain	English, Hindi, French patois, Spanish	Parliamentary democracy; Prime Minister Kamla Persad-Bissessar	1962 / 25	99/98 / 66/73	$21,300 / 0.837
United States	3,717,796 / 309,600,000	79 / 0.6	Washington, D.C.	English, Spanish, others	Presidential-legislative democracy; President Barack Obama	1776 / 20	99/99 / 75/80	$46,000 / 0.956

SOURCES: FOR AREA, POPULATION, URBAN POPULATION, ANNUAL POPULATION INCREASE, PERCENT OF POPULATION UNDER 15 YEARS, AND LIFE EXPECTANCY: *2010 WORLD POPULATION DATA SHEET* (POPULATION REFERENCE BUREAU) • FOR CAPITAL, MAJOR LANGUAGES, DATE OF ORIGIN, LITERACY RATE, AND PER CAPITA GDP: *THE WORLD FACTBOOK 2010* (CENTRAL INTELLIGENCE AGENCY) • FOR POLITICAL SYSTEMS: BASED ON INFORMATION FROM *FREEDOM IN THE WORLD*, AN ANNUAL PUBLICATION OF FREEDOM HOUSE (A NONPROFIT HUMAN-RIGHTS ORGANIZATION) AND ITS WEB SITE (FREEDOMHOUSE.ORG) AND NEWS ACCOUNTS; *WORLD BOOK ENCYCLOPEDIA*; THE U.S. STATE DEPARTMENT AND ITS WEB SITE (STATE.GOV); AND BBC NEWS COUNTRY PROFILES • FOR HEADS OF GOVERNMENT: BASED ON INFORMATION FROM THE GEOCITIES "RULERS" WEB SITE (RULERS.ORG), THE STATE DEPARTMENT AND ITS WEB SITE, *THE WORLD FACTBOOK 2010*, AND NEWS ACCOUNTS • FOR HDI: HUMAN DEVELOPMENT REPORT 2009 (UNITED NATIONS DEVELOPMENT PROGRAM) • FOR KOSOVO: *WORLD BOOK ENCYCLOPEDIA*, *THE WORLD FACTBOOK 2010*, AND THE STATE DEPARTMENT WEB SITE.

DATA COMPILED AND EDITED BY BRYAN BROWN, KATHY WILMORE, VERONICA MAJEROL, MARY HARVEY, AND STEVEN WISHNIA; DATA CONFIRMED AS OF OCTOBER 4, 2010.

SOUTH AMERICA

COUNTRY	AREA (SQ MI) / POPULATION	URBAN POP. % / POP. RISE %/YEAR	CAPITAL	LANGUAGES	POLITICAL SYSTEM & HEAD OF GOVERNMENT	DATE OF ORIGIN / % OF POP. UNDER 15	LITERACY RATE (%) / LIFE EXPECTANCY	PER CAPITA GDP / HDI
Argentina	1,073,514 / 40,500,000	91 / 1.0	Buenos Aires	Spanish, English, Italian, German, French	Presidential-legislative democracy; President Cristina Fernández de Kirchner	1816 / 26	97/97 / 72/79	$13,400 / 0.866
Bolivia	424,162 / 10,400,000	65 / 2.0	La Paz and Sucre	Spanish, Quechua, Aymara	Presidential-legislative democracy; President Evo Morales	1825 / 37	93/81 / 64/68	$4,700 / 0.729
Brazil	3,300,154 / 193,300,000	84 / 1.0	Brasília	Portuguese, Amerindian dialects	Presidential-legislative democracy; President Dilma Rousseff	1822 / 27	88/89 / 69/77	$10,100 / 0.813
Chile	292,135 / 17,100,000	87 / 0.9	Santiago	Spanish	Presidential-legislative democracy; President Sebastián Piñera	1810 / 24	96/96 / 76/82	$14,600 / 0.878
Colombia	439,734 / 45,500,000	75 / 1.4	Bogotá	Spanish	Presidential-legislative democracy; President Juan Manuel Santos	1810 / 30	90/91 / 71/78	$9,200 / 0.807
Ecuador	109,483 / 14,200,000	65 / 1.6	Quito	Spanish, Quechua, Amerindian dialects	Presidential-legislative democracy; President Rafael Correa	1822 / 31	92/90 / 72/78	$7,500 / 0.806
Guyana	83,000 / 800,000	28 / 1.6	Georgetown	English, Amerindian dialects	Presidential-parliamentary democracy; President Bharrat Jagdeo	1966 / 33	92/92 / 62/70	$6,500 / 0.729
Paraguay	157,046 / 6,500,000	58 / 1.9	Asunción	Spanish, Guarani	Presidential-legislative democracy; President Fernando Lugo	1811 / 34	95/93 / 70/74	$4,600 / 0.761
Peru	496,224 / 29,500,000	76 / 1.6	Lima	Spanish, Quechua, Aymara	Presidential-legislative democracy; President Alan García	1821 / 31	96/89 / 71/76	$8,500 / 0.806
Suriname	63,039 / 500,000	67 / 1.3	Paramaribo	Dutch, English, Sranang, Tongo, Hindustani, Javanese	Parliamentary democracy; President Dési Bouterse	1975 / 30	92/87 / 65/73	$9,500 / 0.769
Uruguay	68,498 / 3,400,000	94 / 0.5	Montevideo	Spanish, Portuñol	Presidential-legislative democracy; President José Mujica	1825 / 23	98/98 / 72/80	$12,600 / 0.865
Venezuela	352,143 / 28,800,000	88 / 1.6	Caracas	Spanish, Amerindian dialects	Presidential-legislative democracy; President Hugo Chávez	1811 / 30	93/93 / 71/77	$13,000 / 0.844

EUROPE

COUNTRY	AREA (SQ MI) / POPULATION	URBAN POP. % / POP. RISE %/YEAR	CAPITAL	LANGUAGES	POLITICAL SYSTEM & HEAD OF GOVERNMENT	DATE OF ORIGIN / % OF POP. UNDER 15	LITERACY RATE (%) / LIFE EXPECTANCY	PER CAPITA GDP / HDI
Albania	11,100 / 3,200,000	49 / 0.5	Tirana	Albanian, Greek	Presidential-parliamentary democracy; Prime Minister Sali Berisha	1912 / 25	99/98 / 72/79	$6,400 / 0.818
Andorra	174 / 100,000	90 / 0.7	Andorra la Vella	Catalan, French, Castilian, Portuguese	Presidential-parliamentary democracy; Executive Council President Jaume Bartumeu Cassany	1278 / 14	99/99 / NA	$44,900 / 0.934
Austria	32,378 / 8,400,000	67 / 0	Vienna	German	Parliamentary democracy; Chancellor Werner Faymann	1156 / 15	98 / 78/83	$39,200 / 0.955
Belarus	80,154 / 9,500,000	74 / −0.3	Minsk	Belarusian, Russian, others	Presidential dictatorship; President Aleksandr Lukashenko	1991 / 15	99/99 / 65/76	$12,500 / 0.826
Belgium	11,787 / 10,800,000	99 / 0.2	Brussels	Flemish, French, German	Parliamentary democracy; Prime Minister Yves Leterme	1830 / 17	99/99 / 77/82	$36,800 / 0.953
Bosnia and Herzegovina[2]	19,741 / 3,800,000	46 / 0	Sarajevo	Serbo-Croatian	Presidential-parliamentary (transitional); rotating Chairman of the Presidency[2]	1992 / 16	99/94 / 72/77	$6,400 / 0.812
Bulgaria	42,822 / 7,500,000	71 / −0.4	Sofia	Bulgarian, others	Parliamentary democracy; Prime Minister Boiko Borisov	1908 / 14	99/98 / 70/77	$12,500 / 0.840
Croatia	21,830 / 4,400,000	56 / −0.2	Zagreb	Serbo-Croatian	Presidential-parliamentary democracy; Prime Minister Jadranka Kosor	1991 / 15	99/97 / 72/79	$17,500 / 0.871
Czech Republic	30,448 / 10,500,000	74 / 0.1	Prague	Czech, Slovak	Parliamentary democracy; Prime Minister Petr Nečas	1993 / 14	99/99 / 74/80	$24,900 / 0.903
Denmark	16,637 / 5,500,000	72 / 0.1	Copenhagen	Danish, Greenlandic, Faroese, German	Parliamentary democracy; Prime Minister Lars Løkke Rasmussen	900s / 19	99/99 / 76/81	$36,000 / 0.955

[2]Bosnia and Herzegovina has a collective presidency that alternates among three members (one Croat, one Bosniak Muslim, and one Serb).

COUNTRY	AREA (SQ MI) POPULATION	URBAN POP. % POP. RISE %/YEAR	CAPITAL	LANGUAGES	POLITICAL SYSTEM & HEAD OF GOVERNMENT	DATE OF ORIGIN % OF POP. UNDER 15	LITERACY RATE (%) LIFE EXPECTANCY	PER CAPITA GDP HDI
Estonia	17,413	69	Tallinn	Estonian, Ukrainian, Russian, others	Parliamentary democracy; Prime Minister Andrus Ansip	1991	99/99	$18,500
	1,300,000	0				15	69/79	0.883
Finland	130,560	65	Helsinki	Finnish, Swedish, Lapp, Russian	Presidential-parliamentary democracy; President Tarja Halonen	1917	99/99	$34,100
	5,400,000	0.2				17	77/83	0.959
France	212,934	77	Paris	French, regional dialects	Presidential-parliamentary democracy; President Nicolas Sarkozy	486	99/99	$32,600
	63,000,000	0.4				18	78/85	0.961
Germany	137,830	73	Berlin	German	Parliamentary democracy; Chancellor Angela Merkel	1871	99/99	$34,100
	81,600,000	−0.2				14	77/82	0.947
Greece	50,950	73	Athens	Greek, English, French	Parliamentary democracy; Prime Minister Georgios Papandreou	1829	98/94	$31,000
	11,300,000	0.1				14	77/82	0.942
Hungary	35,919	67	Budapest	Hungarian, others	Parliamentary democracy; Prime Minister Viktor Orbán	1001	99/99	$18,800
	10,000,000	−0.3				15	70/78	0.879
Iceland	39,768	93	Reykjavík	Icelandic	Parliamentary democracy; Prime Minister Jóhanna Sigurdardóttir	1944	99/99	$39,600
	300,000	0.9				21	80/83	0.969
Ireland	27,135	60	Dublin	English, Gaelic	Parliamentary democracy; Prime Minister Brian Cowen	1921	99/99	$41,000
	4,500,000	1.0				21	77/82	0.965
Italy	116,320	68	Rome	Italian, German, French, Slovene	Parliamentary democracy; Prime Minister Silvio Berlusconi	1861	99/98	$29,900
	60,500,000	0				14	79/84	0.951
Kosovo[3]	4,203	NA	Pristina	Albanian, Serbian, others	Presidential-parliamentary democracy (transitional); Prime Minister Hashim Thaçi	2008	97/88	$2,500
	2,300,000	1.4				31	67/71	NA
Latvia	24,942	68	Riga	Lettish, Lithuanian, Russian, others	Parliamentary democracy; Prime Minister Valdis Dombrovskis	1991	99/99	$14,400
	2,200,000	−0.4				14	67/78	0.866
Liechtenstein	62	15	Vaduz	German, Alemannic dialect	Constitutional monarchy; Prince Alois	1719	99/99	$122,100
	40,000	0.4				16	79/82	0.951
Lithuania	25,174	67	Vilnius	Lithuanian, Polish, Russian	Presidential-parliamentary democracy; President Dalia Grybauskaite	1991	99/99	$15,500
	3,300,000	−0.1				15	66/78	0.870
Luxembourg	999	83	Luxembourg	Luxembourgish, German, French, English	Parliamentary democracy; Prime Minister Jean-Claude Juncker	1839	99/99	$79,600
	500,000	0.4				18	78/83	0.960
Macedonia	9,927	65	Skopje	Macedonian, Albanian, others	Presidential-parliamentary democracy; Prime Minister Nikola Gruevski	1991	98/94	$9,100
	2,100,000	0.2				19	71/76	0.817
Malta	124	94	Valletta	Maltese, English	Parliamentary democracy; Prime Minister Lawrence Gonzi	1964	92/94	$24,300
	400,000	0.2				16	77/82	0.902
Moldova	13,012	41	Chisinau	Moldovan, Russian, Gagauz	Parliamentary democracy; Acting President Mihai Ghimpu[4]	1991	99/99	$2,300
	4,100,000	0				17	66/73	0.720
Monaco	1	100	Monaco	French, English, Italian, Monegasque	Constitutional monarchy; Prince Albert II	1419	99/99	$30,000
	40,000	0				13	NA	NA
Montenegro	5,333	64	Podgorica	Montenegrin, Serbian, Bosniak, Albanian	Presidential-parliamentary democracy; President Filip Vujanovic	2006	NA	$9,800
	600,000	0.4				20	71/76	0.834
Netherlands	15,768	66	Amsterdam	Dutch	Parliamentary democracy; Prime Minister Jan Peter Balkenende	1579	99/99	$39,500
	16,600,000	0.3				18	78/82	0.964
Norway	125,050	80	Oslo	Norwegian, Lapp, Finnish	Parliamentary democracy; Prime Minister Jens Stoltenberg	1905	99/99	$57,400
	4,900,000	0.4				19	79/83	0.971
Poland	124,807	61	Warsaw	Polish	Presidential-parliamentary democracy; President Bronislaw Komorowski	1918	99/99	$17,900
	38,200,000	0.1				15	71/80	0.880
Portugal	35,514	55	Lisbon	Portuguese	Presidential-parliamentary democracy; Prime Minister José Sócrates	1140	96/91	$21,700
	10,700,000	−0.1				15	75/82	0.909

[3]Kosovo declared its independence from Serbia on February 17, 2008. As of September 2010, it is recognized by only 70 countries.
[4]Postponed September 2010 elections by Parliament not rescheduled at press time.

EUROPE

COUNTRY	AREA (SQ MI) / POPULATION	URBAN POP. % / POP. RISE %/YEAR	CAPITAL	LANGUAGES	POLITICAL SYSTEM & HEAD OF GOVERNMENT	DATE OF ORIGIN / % OF POP. UNDER 15	LITERACY RATE (%) / LIFE EXPECTANCY	PER CAPITA GDP / HDI
Romania	92,042 / 21,500,000	55 / −0.2	Bucharest	Romanian, Hungarian, German	Presidential-parliamentary democracy; President Traian Basescu	1878 / 15	98/96 / 69/76	$11,500 / 0.837
Russia	6,592,819 / 141,900,000	73 / −0.2	Moscow	Russian, others	Dominant party; President Dmitry Medvedev	1991 / 15	99/99 / 62/74	$15,100 / 0.817
San Marino	23 / 30,000	84 / 0.3	San Marino	Italian	Parliamentary democracy; Co-Captains Regent elected every six months from the Great and General Council	301 / 15	97/95 / 80/86	$41,900 / NA
Serbia	34,115 / 7,300,000	58 / −0.5	Belgrade	Serbo-Croatian, Albanian	Presidential-parliamentary democracy (transitional); President Boris Tadic	1992 / 15	99/94 / 71/76	$10,600 / 0.826
Slovakia	18,923 / 5,400,000	55 / 0.2	Bratislava	Slovak, Hungarian	Parliamentary democracy; Prime Minister Iveta Radicová	1993 / 15	99/99 / 71/79	$21,100 / 0.880
Slovenia	7,819 / 2,100,000	50 / 0.2	Ljubljana	Slovenian, Serbo-Croatian, others	Parliamentary democracy; Prime Minister Borut Pahor	1991 / 14	99/99 / 76/82	$27,700 / 0.929
Spain	195,363 / 47,100,000	77 / 0.3	Madrid	Castilian Spanish, Catalan, Galician, Basque	Parliamentary democracy; Prime Minister José Luis Rodríguez Zapatero	1492 / 15	99/97 / 78/84	$33,600 / 0.955
Sweden	173,730 / 9,400,000	84 / 0.2	Stockholm	Swedish, Lapp, Finnish	Parliamentary democracy; Prime Minister Fredrik Reinfeldt	1523 / 17	99/99 / 79/83	$36,600 / 0.963
Switzerland	15,942 / 7,800,000	73 / 0.2	Bern	German, French, Italian, Romansch, others	Parliamentary democracy; rotating President from seven-member Federal Council	1291 / 15	99/99 / 80/84	$41,400 / 0.960
Ukraine	233,089 / 45,900,000	69 / −0.4	Kiev	Ukrainian, Russian, Romanian, Polish, Hungarian	Presidential-parliamentary democracy; President Viktor Yanukovych	1991 / 14	99/99 / 63/74	$6,300 / 0.796
United Kingdom (England, Scotland, Wales, N. Ireland)	94,548 / 62,200,000	80 / 0.4	London	English, Welsh, Scottish, Gaelic	Parliamentary democracy; Prime Minister David Cameron	circa 900 / 18	99/99 / 77/82	$34,800 / 0.947
Vatican City	109 acres / 826	100 / 0	Vatican City	Italian, Latin, others	Papal state; Pope Benedict XVI	1929 / NA	100 / NA	NA / NA

ASIA

Afghanistan	251,772 / 29,100,000	22 / 2.1	Kabul	Pashtu, Afghan Persian, Turkic, others	Transitional democracy, territory disputed by factions; President Hamid Karzai	1919 / 44	43/13 / 44/44	$1,000 / 0.352
Armenia	11,506 / 3,100,000	64 / 0.6	Yerevan	Armenian, Russian, others	Presidential-parliamentary democracy (transitional); President Serzh Sarkisyan	1991 / 20	99/99 / 68/75	$5,500 / 0.798
Azerbaijan	33,436 / 9,000,000	54 / 1.1	Baku	Azeri, Russian, Armenian, others	Dominant party; President Ilham Aliyev	1991 / 23	99/98 / 70/75	$10,400 / 0.788
Bahrain	266 / 1,300,000	100 / 1.3	Manama	Arabic, English, Farsi, Urdu	Monarchy; King Hamad bin Isa al-Khalifah	1971 / 20	89/84 / 73/77	$38,800 / 0.895
Bangladesh	55,598 / 164,400,000	25 / 1.5	Dhaka	Bengali, English	Presidential-parliamentary (transitional); Prime Minister Sheikh Hasina Wajed	1971 / 32	54/41 / 65/67	$1,500 / 0.543
Bhutan	18,147 / 700,000	32 / 1.7	Thimphu	Dzongkha, Tibetan and Nepalese dialects	Parliamentary democracy in transition from monarchy; Prime Minister Jigmi Thinley	1949 / 31	60/34 / 67/68	$4,700 / 0.619
Brunei	2,228 / 400,000	72 / 1.3	Bandar Seri Begawan	Malay, English, Chinese	Monarchy; Sultan Hassanal Bolkiah	1984 / 27	95/90 / 75/80	$51,200 / 0.920
Cambodia	69,900 / 15,100,000	20 / 1.6	Phnom Penh	Khmer, French	Dominant party; Prime Minister Hun Sen	1949 / 35	85/64 / 59/63	$1,900 / 0.593
China	3,696,100 / 1,338,100,000	47 / 0.5	Beijing	Mandarin, other Chinese languages, other languages	One-party dictatorship; President Hu Jintao	1912 / 18	96/88 / 72/76	$6,600 / 0.772
Cyprus[5]	3,571 / 1,100,000	62 / 0.6	Nicosia	Greek, Turkish, English	Presidential-parliamentary democracy; President Dimitris Christofias	1960 / 18	99/96 / 77/80	$21,000 / 0.914

5 Does not include separate Turkish Cypriot-controlled area in north.

COUNTRY	AREA (SQ MI) POPULATION	URBAN POP. % POP. RISE %/YEAR	CAPITAL	LANGUAGES	POLITICAL SYSTEM & HEAD OF GOVERNMENT	DATE OF ORIGIN % OF POP. UNDER 15	LITERACY RATE (%) LIFE EXPECTANCY	PER CAPITA GDP HDI
Georgia	26,911 / 4,600,000	53 / 0.3	Tbilisi	Georgian, Russian, Armenian, Azeri, Ossetian, others	Presidential-parliamentary democracy; President Mikheil Saakashvili	1991 / 17	99/99 / 69/79	$4,400 / 0.778
India	1,269,340 / 1,188,800,000	29 / 1.5	New Delhi	Hindi, English, Bengali, many others	Parliamentary democracy; Prime Minister Manmohan Singh	1947 / 32	73/48 / 63/65	$3,100 / 0.612
Indonesia	735,355 / 235,500,000	43 / 1.4	Jakarta	Bahasa Indonesian, English, Dutch, others	Parliamentary democracy; President Susilo Bambang Yudhoyono	1945 / 28	94/87 / 69/73	$4,000 / 0.734
Iran	630,575 / 75,100,000	69 / 1.3	Tehran	Farsi, Turkic, Kurdish, Luri, others	Presidential-parliamentary under religious control; President Mahmoud Ahmadinejad	1502 / 28	84/70 / 70/73	$12,500 / 0.782
Iraq	169,236 / 31,500,000	67 / 2.6	Baghdad	Arabic, Kurdish, Assyrian, Armenian	Transitional to parliamentary democracy; Prime Minister Nuri al-Maliki	1932 / 41	84/64 / 64/72	$3,800 / NA
Israel[6]	8,131 / 7,600,000	92 / 1.6	Jerusalem	Hebrew, Arabic, English	Parliamentary democracy; Prime Minister Benjamin Netanyahu	1948 / 28	99/96 / 79/83	$28,400 / 0.935
Japan	145,869 / 127,400,000	86 / 0	Tokyo	Japanese	Parliamentary democracy; Prime Minister Naoto Kan	660 B.C. / 13	99/99 / 79/86	$32,700 / 0.960
Jordan	34,444 / 6,500,000	83 / 2.6	Amman	Arabic, English	Constitutional monarchy; King Abdullah II	1946 / 37	95/85 / 72/74	$5,200 / 0.770
Kazakhstan	1,049,151 / 16,300,000	54 / 1.4	Astana	Kazakh, Russian, Ukrainian, others	Dominant party; President Nursultan Nazarbayev	1991 / 24	99/99 / 63/74	$11,800 / 0.804
Korea, North	46,541 / 22,800,000	60 / 0.5	Pyongyang	Korean	Communist dictatorship; General Secretary Kim Jong Il	1945 / 22	99/99 / 61/66	$1,900 / NA
Korea, South	38,324 / 48,900,000	82 / 0.4	Seoul	Korean, English	Presidential-parliamentary democracy; President Lee Myung Bak	1945 / 17	99/97 / 77/83	$28,100 / 0.937
Kuwait	6,880 / 3,100,000	98 / 2.0	Kuwait	Arabic, English	Monarchy; Emir Sabah al-Ahmad al-Jabir al-Sabah	1961 / 23	94/91 / 76/80	$52,800 / 0.916
Kyrgyzstan	76,641 / 5,300,000	35 / 1.6	Bishkek	Kirghiz, Russian	Presidential-parliamentary (transitional after coup); Interim President Roza Otunbayeva	1991 / 29	99/98 / 64/72	$2,200 / 0.710
Laos	91,429 / 6,400,000	27 / 2.1	Vientiane	Lao, French, English, others	Communist one-party state; President Choummaly Sayasone	1949 / 39	83/63 / 63/66	$2,100 / 0.619
Lebanon	4,015 / 4,300,000	87 / 1.5	Beirut	Arabic, French, Armenian, English	Presidential-parliamentary democracy; President Michel Suleiman	1943 / 25	93/82 / 70/74	$13,200 / 0.803
Malaysia	127,317 / 28,900,000	63 / 1.6	Kuala Lumpur	Malay, English, Chinese languages, many others	Dominant party; Prime Minister Najib Tun Razak	1957 / 32	92/85 / 72/77	$14,900 / 0.829
Maldives	116 / 300,000	35 / 1.9	Malé	Maldivian Divehi, English	Presidential-parliamentary democracy (transitional); President Mohamed Nasheed	1965 / 30	96/96 / 72/74	$4,300 / 0.771
Mongolia	604,826 / 2,800,000	60 / 1.9	Ulaanbaatar	Khalkha Mongolian, Turkic, Russian, Chinese	Presidential-parliamentary democracy; Prime Minister Sükhbaataryn Batbold	1921 / 33	98/98 / 63/70	$3,100 / 0.727
Myanmar (Burma)	261,228 / 53,400,000	31 / 0.9	Naypyidaw Myodaw	Burmese, others	Military rule; General Than Shwe	1948 / 27	94/86 / 56/60	$1,100 / 0.586
Nepal	56,826 / 28,000,000	17 / 1.9	Kathmandu	Nepali, others	Parliamentary democracy (transitional from monarchy); Prime Minister Jhalanath Khanal	1768 / 37	63/35 / 64/65	$1,200 / 0.553
Oman	82,031 / 3,100,000	72 / 1.8	Muscat	Arabic, English, Baluchi, Urdu, others	Monarchy; Sultan Qaboos bin Said al-Said	1650 / 29	87/74 / 70/74	$25,000 / 0.846
Pakistan	307,375 / 184,800,000	35 / 2.3	Islamabad	Urdu, Punjabi, Sindhi, Siraiki, English, others	Presidential-parliamentary (transitional from military); President Asif Ali Zardari	1947 / 38	63/36 / 66/67	$2,500 / 0.572
Philippines	115,830 / 94,000,000	63 / 2.1	Manila	Filipino, English	Presidential-legislative democracy; President Benigno Aquino III	1898 / 33	93/93 / 70/74	$3,300 / 0.751

ASIA

COUNTRY	AREA (SQ MI) / POPULATION	URBAN POP. % / POP. RISE %/YEAR	CAPITAL	LANGUAGES	POLITICAL SYSTEM & HEAD OF GOVERNMENT	DATE OF ORIGIN / % OF POP. UNDER 15	LITERACY RATE (%) / LIFE EXPECTANCY	PER CAPITA GDP / HDI
Qatar	4,247 / 1,700,000	100 / 0.8	Doha	Arabic, English	Monarchy; Emir Hamad bin Khalifa al-Thani	1971 / 15	89/89 / 75/77	$119,500 / 0.910
Saudi Arabia	829,996 / 29,200,000	81 / 2.6	Riyadh	Arabic	Monarchy; King Abdallah bin Abd al-Aziz Al Saud	1932 / 38	85/71 / 74/78	$20,600 / 0.843
Singapore	239 / 5,100,000	100 / 0.6	Singapore	Chinese, Malay, Tamil, English	Dominant party; Prime Minister Lee Hsien Loong	1965 / 18	97/89 / 79/84	$52,200 / 0.944
Sri Lanka	25,332 / 20,700,000	15 / 1.2	Colombo	Tamil, Sinhala, English	Presidential-parliamentary democracy; President Mahinda Rajapakse	1948 / 26	92/89 / 72/76	$4,500 / 0.759
Syria	71,498 / 22,500,000	54 / 2.5	Damascus	Arabic, Kurdish, Armenian, French, others	Dominant party; President Bashar al-Assad	1946 / 36	86/74 / 72/76	$4,600 / 0.742
Taiwan	13,969 / 23,200,000	78 / 0.2	Taipei	Mandarin Chinese, Taiwanese, others	Presidential-parliamentary democracy; President Ma Ying-jeou	1949 / 16	96 / 75/82	$32,000 / NA
Tajikistan	55,251 / 7,600,000	26 / 2.4	Dushanbe	Tajik, Russian	Dominant party; President Emomalii Rakhmon	1991 / 38	99/99 / 64/69	$1,900 / 0.688
Thailand	198,116 / 68,100,000	31 / 0.6	Bangkok	Thai, English, regional dialects	Transitional after military coup; Prime Minister Abhisit Vejjajiva	1238 / 22	95/91 / 66/72	$8,200 / 0.783
Timor-Leste (East Timor)	5,741 / 1,200,000	22 / 3.1	Dili	Tetun, Portuguese, Indonesian, English	Presidential-parliamentary democracy (transitional); Prime Minister Xanana Gusmão	2002 / 45	59 / 60/62	$2,400 / 0.489
Turkey	299,158 / 73,600,000	76 / 1.2	Ankara	Turkish, Kurdish, Arabic	Parliamentary democracy; Prime Minister Recep Tayyip Erdogan	1923 / 26	95/80 / 69/74	$11,400 / 0.806
Turkmenistan	188,456 / 5,200,000	47 / 1.4	Ashgabat	Turkmen, Uzbek, Russian, others	Presidential dictatorship; President Gurbanguly Berdymukhammedov	1991 / 31	99/98 / 61/69	$6,700 / 0.739
United Arab Emirates	32,278 / 5,400,000	83 / 1.4	Abu Dhabi	Arabic, Farsi, English, Hindi, Urdu	Federation of traditional monarchies; President Khalifa bin Zayid al-Nuhayyan	1971 / 19	76/82 / 77/79	$38,900 / 0.903
Uzbekistan	172,741 / 28,100,000	36 / 1.8	Tashkent	Uzbek, Russian, Tajik, others	Presidential dictatorship; President Islam Karimov	1991 / 33	99/99 / 65/71	$2,800 / 0.710
Vietnam	128,066 / 88,900,000	28 / 1.2	Hanoi	Vietnamese, French, Chinese, English, Khmer, others	Communist one-party state; Prime Minister Nguyen Tan Dung	1945 / 25	94/87 / 72/76	$2,900 / 0.725
Yemen	203,849 / 23,600,000	29 / 3.0	Sanaa	Arabic	Dominant party; President Ali Abdullah Saleh	1990 / 45	71/30 / 62/64	$2,500 / 0.575

OCEANIA

COUNTRY	AREA (SQ MI) / POPULATION	URBAN POP. % / POP. RISE %/YEAR	CAPITAL	LANGUAGES	POLITICAL SYSTEM & HEAD OF GOVERNMENT	DATE OF ORIGIN / % OF POP. UNDER 15	LITERACY RATE (%) / LIFE EXPECTANCY	PER CAPITA GDP / HDI
Australia	2,988,888 / 22,400,000	82 / 0.7	Canberra	English, aboriginal languages	Parliamentary democracy; Prime Minister Julia Gillard	1901 / 19	99/99 / 79/84	$40,000 / 0.970
Fiji	7,054 / 900,000	51 / 1.7	Suva	English, Fijian, Hindustani	Military; Interim Prime Minister Commodore Voreqe Bainimarama	1970 / 29	96/92 / 66/71	$3,900 / 0.741
Kiribati	282 / 100,000	44 / 1.8	Tarawa	English, Gilbertese	Presidential-legislative democracy; President Anote Tong	1979 / 36	NA / 59/63	$6,100 / NA
Marshall Islands	69 / 100,000	68 / 2.8	Majuro	English, Marshallese dialects, Japanese	Parliamentary democracy and traditional chiefs; President Jurelang Zedkaia	1986 / 41	94/94 / 64/67	$2,500 / NA
Micronesia	270 / 100,000	22 / 1.9	Palikir	English, Trukese, Pohnpein, Yapese, Kosraean	Parliamentary democracy; President Emanuel Mori	1986 / 37	91/88 / 67/68	$2,200 / NA
Nauru	9 / 10,000	100 / 1.9	Yaren District	Nauruan, English	Parliamentary democracy; Interim President Marcus Stephen (during state of emergency)	1968 / 39	NA / 55/57	$5,000 / NA

OCEANIA

COUNTRY	AREA (SQ MI) / POPULATION	URBAN POP. % / POP. RISE %/YEAR	CAPITAL	LANGUAGES	POLITICAL SYSTEM & HEAD OF GOVERNMENT	DATE OF ORIGIN / % OF POP. UNDER 15	LITERACY RATE (%) / LIFE EXPECTANCY	PER CAPITA GDP / HDI
New Zealand	104,452 / 4,400,000	86 / 0.8	Wellington	English, Maori	Parliamentary democracy; Prime Minister John Key	1907 / 21	99/99 / 78/82	$27,400 / 0.950
Palau	178 / 20,000	78 / 0.6	Melekeok	English, Sonsorolese, Palauan, others	Presidential-legislative democracy and traditional chiefs; President Johnson Toribiong	1994 / 24	93/90 / 66/72	$8,100 / NA
Papua New Guinea	178,703 / 6,800,000	13 / 2.2	Port Moresby	English, pidgin English, Motu, many others	Parliamentary democracy; Prime Minister Sir Michael Somare	1975 / 40	63/51 / 57/62	$2,300 / 0.541
Samoa	1,097 / 200,000	22 / 2.0	Apia	Samoan, English	Parliamentary democracy and traditional chiefs; Prime Minister Tuilaepa Sailele Malielegaoi	1962 / 40	99/99 / 72/74	$5,400 / 0.771
Solomon Islands	11,158 / 500,000	17 / 2.5	Honiara	Melanesian pidgin, English, others	Parliamentary democracy; Prime Minister Danny Philip	1978 / 41	NA / 62/63	$2,500 / 0.610
Tonga	290 / 100,000	23 / 2.2	Nuku'alofa	Tongan, English	Monarchy; King George Tupou V	1970 / 38	99/99 / 67/73	$6,300 / 0.768
Tuvalu	10 / 10,000	47 / 1.4	Funafuti	Tuvaluan, English	Parliamentary democracy; Prime Minister Willy Telavi	1978 / 32	NA / 62/65	$1,600 / NA
Vanuatu	4,707 / 200,000	24 / 2.5	Port-Vila	English, French, Bislama	Parliamentary democracy; Prime Minister Edward Natapei	1980 / 40	74 / 66/69	$5,300 / 0.693

AFRICA

COUNTRY	AREA (SQ MI) / POPULATION	URBAN POP. % / POP. RISE %/YEAR	CAPITAL	LANGUAGES	POLITICAL SYSTEM & HEAD OF GOVERNMENT	DATE OF ORIGIN / % OF POP. UNDER 15	LITERACY RATE (%) / LIFE EXPECTANCY	PER CAPITA GDP / HDI
Algeria	919,591 / 36,000,000	63 / 1.8	Algiers	Arabic, French, Berber dialects	Dominant party; Government in transition	1962 / 28	80/60 / 71/74	$7,100 / 0.754
Angola	481,351 / 19,000,000	57 / 2.5	Luanda	Portuguese, Bantu, others	Presidential-parliamentary (transitional); President José Eduardo dos Santos	1975 / 45	83/54 / 45/49	$8,400 / 0.564
Benin	43,483 / 9,800,000	41 / 3.0	Porto-Novo	French, Fon, Yoruba, others	Presidential-legislative democracy; President Yayi Boni	1960 / 45	48/23 / 57/60	$1,500 / 0.492
Botswana	224,606 / 1,800,000	60 / 1.9	Gaborone	English, Setswana	Parliamentary democracy and traditional chiefs; President Ian Khama	1966 / 33	80/82 / 55/55	$12,800 / 0.694
Burkina Faso	105,792 / 16,200,000	23 / 3.4	Ouagadougou	French, Sudanic languages	Presidential-parliamentary democracy (transitional); President Blaise Compaoré	1960 / 46	29/15 / 51/54	$1,200 / 0.389
Burundi	10,745 / 8,500,000	10 / 2.1	Bujumbura	Kirundi, French, Swahili	Presidential-legislative democracy (transitional); President Pierre Nkurunziza	1962 / 41	67/52 / 49/52	$300 / 0.394
Cameroon	183,568 / 20,000,000	53 / 2.3	Yaoundé	English, French, African languages	Dominant party; President Paul Biya	1960 / 41	77/60 / 50/52	$2,300 / 0.523
Cape Verde	1,556 / 500,000	61 / 2.0	Praia	Portuguese, Crioulo	Presidential-parliamentary democracy; Prime Minister José Maria Neves	1975 / 35	86/69 / 69/76	$3,600 / 0.708
Central African Republic	240,533 / 4,800,000	38 / 2.2	Bangui	French, Sangho, Arabic, Hunsa, Swahili	Presidential-parliamentary democracy (transitional); President François Bozizé	1960 / 41	65/34 / 47/50	$700 / 0.369
Chad	495,753 / 11,500,000	27 / 2.9	N'Djamena	French, Arabic, Sara, others	Dominant party; President Idriss Déby	1960 / 46	41/13 / 47/50	$1,900 / 0.392
Comoros	861 / 700,000	28 / 2.6	Moroni	Arabic, French, Comoran	Presidential-parliamentary; President Elect Ikililou Dhoinine	1975 / 38	64/49 / 62/66	$1,000 / 0.576
Congo, Democratic Republic	905,351 / 67,800,000	33 / 2.9	Kinshasa	French, Lingala, Kingwana, Kikongo, Tshiluba	In transition from military to presidential-parliamentary; President Joseph Kabila	1960 / 48	81/54 / 46/49	$300 / 0.389
Congo, Republic	132,046 / 3,900,000	60 / 2.5	Brazzaville	French, Lingala, Mono-kutuba, Kikongo, others	Military (transitional); President Denis Sassou-Nguesso	1960 / 42	90/78 / 52/54	$3,900 / 0.601

COUNTRY	AREA (SQ MI)	URBAN POP. %	CAPITAL	LANGUAGES	POLITICAL SYSTEM & HEAD OF GOVERNMENT	DATE OF ORIGIN	LITERACY RATE (%)	PER CAPITA GDP
POPULATION		POP. RISE %/YEAR				% OF POP. UNDER 15	LIFE EXPECTANCY	HDI
Côte d'Ivoire (Ivory Coast)	124,502	50	Yamoussoukro	French, Dioula, others	Presidential-parliamentary (transitional); President Laurent Gbagbo	1960	61/39	$1,700
22,000,000		2.4				40	51/54	0.484
Djibouti	8,958	76	Djibouti	French, Arabic, Somali, Afar	President Ismail Omar Guelleh	1977	78/58	$2,700
900,000		1.8				37	54/57	0.520
Egypt	386,660	43	Cairo	Arabic, English, French	Government in transition	1922	83/59	$6,000
80,400,000		2.1				33	69/75	0.703
Equatorial Guinea	10,830	39	Malabo	Spanish, French, pidgin English, Fang, Bubi, Ibo	Presidential dictatorship; President Teodoro Obiang Nguema Mbasogo	1968	93/81	$37,500
700,000		2.3				42	48/51	0.719
Eritrea	45,405	21	Asmara	Amharic, Arabic, Afar, Tigrinya, Tigre, many others	One-party dictatorship; President Isaias Afewerki	1993	70/48	$700
5,200,000		2.9				42	57/62	0.472
Ethiopia	426,371	16	Addis Ababa	Amharic, Tigrinya, Arabic, Orominga, English, others	Dominant party; Prime Minister Meles Zenawi	1000 B.C.	50/35	$900
85,000,000		2.7				44	54/57	0.414
Gabon	103,347	84	Libreville	French, Fang, Myene, Bateke, others	Dominant party; President Ali Ondimba Bongo	1965	48/33	$14,000
1,500,000		1.9				43	54/57	0.456
Gambia	4,363	54	Banjul	English, Mandinka, Wolof, Fula, others	Dominant party; President Yahya Jammeh	1965	48/33	$1,400
1,800,000		2.7				43	54/57	0.456
Ghana	92,100	48	Accra	English, Akan, others	Presidential-parliamentary democracy; President John Atta Mills	1957	66/50	$1,500
24,000,000		2.2				39	58/61	0.526
Guinea	94,927	28	Conakry	French, various African languages	Republic; President Alpha Condé	1958	43/18	$1,000
10,800,000		3.0				43	55/58	0.435
Guinea-Bissau	13,946	30	Bissau	Portuguese, Criolo, others	Presidential-legislative (transitional); President Malam Bacai Sanhá	1973	58/27	$1,100
1,600,000		2.4				43	45/48	0.396
Kenya	224,081	18	Nairobi	English, Swahili, many others	Presidential-parliamentary democracy; President Mwai Kibaki	1963	91/80	$1,600
40,000,000		2.7				42	56/57	0.541
Lesotho	11,718	23	Maseru	Sesotho, English, Zulu, Xhosa	Parliamentary and traditional chiefs (transitional); Prime Minister Pakalitha Mosisili	1966	75/95	$1,600
1,900,000		0.9				34	40/43	0.514
Liberia	43,000	58	Monrovia	English, Niger-Congo languages	Presidential-parliamentary democracy (transitional); President Ellen Johnson-Sirleaf	1847	73/42	$400
4,100,000		3.3				44	54/57	0.442
Libya	679,359	77	Tripoli	Arabic, Italian, English	Dictatorship; Colonel Muammar al-Qaddafi	1951	92/72	$13,400
6,500,000		1.9				30	72/77	0.847
Madagascar	226,656	31	Antananarivo	French, Malagasy	Presidential-parliamentary democracy (transitional); President Andry Rajoelina	1960	76/63	$1,000
20,100,000		2.7				43	59/62	0.543
Malawi	45,745	14	Lilongwe	English, Chichewa, others	Presidential-legislative democracy; President Bingu wa Mutharika	1964	76/50	$800
15,400,000		2.9				46	48/50	0.493
Mali	478,838	33	Bamako	French, Bambara, many others	Presidential-parliamentary democracy; President Amadou Toumani Touré	1960	54/40	$1,200
15,200,000		3.1				48	50/53	0.371
Mauritania	395,954	40	Nouakchott	Hasaniya Arabic, Pulaar, Soninke, Wolof, French	Presidential-legislative (transitional); President Mohamed Ould Abdel Aziz	1960	60/43	$2,000
3,400,000		2.3				40	55/59	0.520
Mauritius	788	42	Port Louis	English, Creole, French, Hindi, Urdu, Hakka, Bojpoori	Parliamentary democracy; Prime Minister Navin Ramgoolam	1968	88/81	$13,000
1,300,000		0.5				22	69/76	0.804
Morocco	172,413	57	Rabat	Arabic, Berber dialects, French	Constitutional monarchy; King Muhammad VI	1956	66/40	$4,700
31,900,000		1.5				29	69/73	0.654
Mozambique	309,494	31	Maputo	Portuguese, African languages	Presidential-parliamentary democracy; President Armando Guebuza	1975	64/33	$900
23,400,000		2.3				44	47/49	0.402
Namibia	318,259	35	Windhoek	Afrikaans, German, English, local African languages	Presidential-parliamentary democracy; President Hifikepunye Pohamba	1990	87/84	$6,600
2,200,000		1.9				38	60/62	0.686

AFRICA

COUNTRY	AREA (SQ MI) / POPULATION	URBAN POP. % / POP. RISE %/YEAR	CAPITAL	LANGUAGES	POLITICAL SYSTEM & HEAD OF GOVERNMENT	DATE OF ORIGIN / % OF POP. UNDER 15	LITERACY RATE (%) / LIFE EXPECTANCY	PER CAPITA GDP / HDI
Niger	489,189	20	Niamey	French, Hausa, Djerma	Military (transitional); Chairman Salou Djibo	1960	43/15	$700
	15,900,000	3.5				49	48/49	0.340
Nigeria	356,668	47	Abuja	English, Hausa, Yoruba, Ibo, Fulani	Presidential-legislative democracy; President Goodluck Jonathan	1960	76/61	$2,300
	158,300,000	2.4				43	47/48	0.511
Rwanda	10,170	17	Kigali	Kinyarwanda, French, English, Kiswahili	Dominant party; President Paul Kagame	1962	76/65	$1,000
	10,400,000	2.9				42	50/53	0.460
São Tomé and Príncipe	371	58	São Tomé	Portuguese	Presidential-parliamentary democracy; President Fradique de Menezes	1975	92/78	$1,700
	200,000	2.9				44	64/69	0.651
Senegal	75,954	41	Dakar	French, Wolof, Pulaar, Diola, Mandingo	Presidential-parliamentary democracy; President Abdoulaye Wade	1960	51/29	$1,600
	12,500,000	2.8				44	54/57	0.464
Seychelles	174	53	Victoria	English, French, Creole	Presidential-legislative democracy; President James Michel	1976	91/92	$20,800
	100,000	1.0				22	68/78	0.845
Sierra Leone	27,699	36	Freetown	English, Mende, Temne, Krio	Presidential-legislative democracy; President Ernest Bai Koroma	1961	47/24	$900
	5,800,000	2.4				43	46/49	0.365
Somalia	246,201	34	Mogadishu	Somali, Arabic, Italian, English	Limited government disputed by factions	1960	50/26	$600
	9,400,000	3.0				45	48/51	NA
South Africa	471,444	52	Cape Town, Pretoria, and Bloemfontein	English, Afrikaans, Zulu, Xhosa, Swazi, Sotho, others	Parliamentary democracy; President Jacob Zuma	1910	87/86	$10,300
	49,900,000	0.9				31	54/57	0.683
Sudan	967,494	38	Khartoum	Arabic, Nubian, Ta Bedawie, English, others	Presidential-legislative (military-dominated); President Omar Hassan Ahmad al-Bashir	1956	72/51	$2,300
	43,200,000	2.2				41	57/60	0.531
Swaziland	6,703	22	Mbabane and Lobamba	English, siSwati	Monarchy; King Mswati III	1968	83/81	$4,400
	1,200,000	1.5				40	46/45	0.572
Tanzania	364,900	25	Dar es Salaam	Kiswahili, English, Arabic, many others	Dominant party; President Jakaya Kikwete	1964	78/62	$1,400
	45,000,000	3.0				45	55/56	0.530
Togo	21,927	40	Lomé	French, Ewe, Mina, Dagomba, Kabye	Dominant party; President Faure Gnassingbé	1960	75/47	$900
	6,800,000	2.5				41	60/63	0.499
Tunisia	63,170	66	Tunis	Arabic, French	Dominant party; President Zine El Abidine Ben Ali	1956	83/65	$8,200
	10,500,000	1.2				24	72/76	0.769
Uganda	93,066	13	Kampala	English, Luganda, Swahili, others	Dominant party; President Yoweri Museveni	1962	77/58	$1,200
	33,800,000	3.4				49	52/53	0.514
Zambia	290,583	37	Lusaka	English, Bemba, Tonga, others	Presidential-legislative democracy (transitional); President Rupiah Banda	1964	87/75	$1,600
	13,300,000	2.5				46	41/42	0.481
Zimbabwe	150,873	37	Harare	English, Shona, Sindebele, others	Dominant party; President Robert Mugabe	1980	94/87	$100
	12,600,000	1.3				42	41/44	NA

THE MIDDLE EAST

COUNTRY	AREA (SQ MI) / POPULATION	URBAN POP. % / POP. RISE %/YEAR	CAPITAL	LANGUAGES	POLITICAL SYSTEM & HEAD OF GOVERNMENT	DATE OF ORIGIN / % OF POP. UNDER 15	LITERACY RATE (%) / LIFE EXPECTANCY	PER CAPITA GDP / HDI
Bahrain	266	100	Manama	Arabic, English, Farsi, Urdu	Monarchy; King Hamad bin Isa al-Khalifah	1971	89/84	$38,800
	1,300,000	1.3				20	73/77	0.895
Cyprus[7]	3,571	62	Nicosia	Greek, Turkish, English	Presidential-parliamentary (divided); Presidents Dimitris Christofias and Dervis Eroglu	1960	99/96	$21,000
	1,100,000	0.6				18	77/80	0.914
Egypt	386,660	43	Cairo	Arabic, English, French	Government in transition	1922	83/59	$6,000
	80,400,000	2.1				33	69/75	0.703
Iran	630,575	69	Tehran	Farsi, Turkic, Kurdish, Luri, others	Presidential-parliamentary under religious control; President Mahmoud Ahmadinejad	1502	84/70	$12,500
	75,100,000	1.3				28	70/73	0.782

[7] Does not include separate Turkish Cypriot-controlled area in the north.

COUNTRY	AREA (SQ MI) / POPULATION	URBAN POP. % / POP. RISE %/YEAR	CAPITAL	LANGUAGES	POLITICAL SYSTEM & HEAD OF GOVERNMENT	DATE OF ORIGIN / % OF POP. UNDER 15	LITERACY RATE (%) / LIFE EXPECTANCY	PER CAPITA GDP / HDI
Iraq	169,236	67	Baghdad	Arabic, Kurdish, Assyrian, Armenian	Transitional to parliamentary democracy; results of March 2010 elections disputed at press time	1932	84/64	$3,800
	31,500,000	2.6				41	64/72	NA
Israel[8]	8,131	92	Jerusalem	Hebrew, Arabic, English	Parliamentary democracy; Prime Minister Benjamin Netanyahu	1948	99/96	$28,400
	7,600,000	1.6				28	79/83	0.935
Jordan	34,444	83	Amman	Arabic, English	Constitutional monarchy; King Abdullah II	1946	95/85	$5,200
	6,500,000	2.6				38	72/74	0.770
Kuwait	6,880	98	Kuwait	Arabic, English	Monarchy; Emir Sheikh Sabah al-Ahmad al-Jabir al-Sabah	1961	94/91	$52,800
	3,100,000	2.0				23	76/80	0.916
Lebanon	4,015	87	Beirut	Arabic, French, Armenian, English	Presidential-parliamentary democracy; President Michel Suleiman	1943	93/82	$13,200
	4,300,000	1.5				25	70/74	0.803
Oman	82,031	72	Muscat	Arabic, English, Baluchi, Urdu, others	Monarchy; Sultan Qaboos bin Said al-Said	1650	87/74	$25,000
	3,100,000	1.8				29	70/74	0.846
Qatar	4,247	100	Doha	Arabic, English	Monarchy; Emir Hamid bin Khalifa al-Thani	1971	89/89	$119,500
	1,700,000	0.8				15	75/77	0.910
Saudi Arabia	829,996	81	Riyadh	Arabic	Monarchy; King Abdallah bin Abd al-Aziz Al Saud	1932	85/71	$20,600
	29,200,000	2.6				38	74/78	0.843
Syria	71,498	54	Damascus	Arabic, Kurdish, Armenian, French, others	Dominant party; President Bashar al-Assad	1946	86/74	$4,600
	22,500,000	2.5				36	72/76	0.742
Turkey	299,158	76	Ankara	Turkish, Kurdish, Arabic	Parliamentary democracy; Prime Minister Recep Tayyip Erdogan	1923	95/80	$11,400
	73,600,000	1.2				26	69/74	0.806
United Arab Emirates	32,278	83	Abu Dhabi	Arabic, Farsi, English, Hindi, Urdu	Federation of traditional monarchies; President Khalifa bin Zayid al-Nuhayyan	1971	76/82	$38,900
	5,400,000	1.4				19	77/79	0.903
Yemen	203,849	29	Sanaa	Arabic	Dominant party; President Ali Abdullah Saleh	1990	71/30	$2,500
	23,600,000	3.0				45	62/64	0.575

8 Does not include Israeli-occupied parts of the West Bank.

The U.S. in Focus, Part 1

You live in the U.S., but how much do you know about it? Who are the movers and shakers who head the federal government's three branches? Which of the 50 states has a name that means "sky-tinted waters"? What territory did the U.S. buy from Denmark for $25 million?

If you don't know the answers off the top of your head, no problem. They are all in this table. These five pages provide a wealth of information about the 50 states, the District of Columbia, and U.S. territories and commonwealths. Happy exploring!

Area: 3,536,338 square miles; ranks fourth* in the world.

Population: 310,929,002; ranks third** in the world.

Capital: Washington, D.C.

Form of Government: Presidential-legislative democracy. The U.S. Constitution divides federal (national) powers among three independent branches of government: the legislative, the executive, and the judicial. Powers not given to the federal government by the Constitution are held by the states.

*After Russia, China, and Canada. **After China and India.

STATE NAME / NICKNAME	ORIGIN OF NAME	ENTERED UNION	LAND AREA (SQ MI) / POPULATION[1]	CAPITAL	GOVERNOR	U.S. SENATORS	U.S. REPS.
ALABAMA The Yellowhammer State	Named for the Alibamu Indian tribe	1819	51,718 4,708,708	Montgomery	Robert Bentley, R	2R	1D 6R
ALASKA The Last Frontier	Russian version of an Aleut word meaning *great land*	1959	587,878 698,473	Juneau	Sean Parnell, R	1D 1R	1R
ARIZONA The Grand Canyon State	Indian word *arizonac*, which means *small spring*	1912	114,007 6,595,778	Phoenix	Jan Brewer, R	2R	3D 5R
ARKANSAS The Natural State	From an Indian word meaning *land of downstream people*	1836	53,183 2,889,450	Little Rock	Mike Beebe, D	1D 1R	1D 3R
CALIFORNIA The Golden State	Named after a treasure island in a popular Spanish tale	1850	158,648 36,961,664	Sacramento	Jerry Brown, D	2D	34D 19R
COLORADO The Centennial State	Spanish for *colored red*	1876	104,100 5,024,748	Denver	John Hickenlooper, D	2D	3D 4R
CONNECTICUT The Constitution State	Algonquian word that means *on the long tidal river*	1788	5,006 3,518,288	Hartford	Dan Malloy, D	1D 1 Ind[2]	5D
DELAWARE The First State	Honors Lord De La Warr, first Governor of Virginia	1787	2,026 885,122	Dover	Jack Markell, D	2D	1D
FLORIDA The Sunshine State	Spanish word meaning *flowery*	1845	58,681 18,537,969	Tallahassee	Rick Scott, R	1D 1R	6D 19R
GEORGIA The Peach State	Honors King George II of Great Britain	1788	58,930 9,829,211	Atlanta	Nathan Deal, R	2R	5D 8R
HAWAII The Aloha State	Named in honor of Polynesian Chief Hawaii-loa	1959	6,459 1,295,178	Honolulu	Neil Abercrombie, D	2D	2D
IDAHO The Gem State	Word invented by settlers; the meaning is unknown	1890	83,574 1,545,801	Boise	C. L. "Butch" Otter, R	2R	2R
ILLINOIS The Prairie State	For the Illiniwek Indians; the name means *superior men*	1818	56,343 12,910,409	Springfield	Pat Quinn, D	1D 1R	8D 11R
INDIANA The Hoosier State	The name means *land of Indians*	1816	36,185 6,423,113	Indianapolis	Mitch Daniels, R	2R	3D 6R
IOWA The Hawkeye State	Indian word for *beautiful land*	1846	56,276 3,007,856	Des Moines	Terry Branstad, R	1D 1R	3D 2R

STATE NAME / NICKNAME	ORIGIN OF NAME	ENTERED UNION	LAND AREA (SQ MI) / POPULATION[1]	CAPITAL	GOVERNOR	U.S. SENATORS	U.S. REPS.
KANSAS The Sunflower State	For the Kansa Indians; the name means *people of the south wind*	1861	82,282 2,818,747	**Topeka**	Sam Brownback, R	2R	4R
KENTUCKY The Bluegrass State	Cherokee word for *meadowland*	1792	40,411 4,314,113	**Frankfort**	Steven Beshear, D	2R	2D 4R
LOUISIANA The Pelican State	Honors Louis XIV, King of France	1812	47,717 4,492,076	**Baton Rouge**	Bobby Jindal, R	1D 1R	1D 6R
MAINE The Pine Tree State	Named by English explorers; name is short for *mainland*	1820	33,128 1,318,301	**Augusta**	Paul LePage, R	2R	2D
MARYLAND The Old Line State; The Free State	Honors Queen Henrietta Maria of England	1788	10,455 5,699,478	**Annapolis**	Martin O'Malley, D	2D	6D 2R
MASSACHUSETTS The Bay State	For the Massachusett Indians; the name means *near the great hill*	1788	8,262 6,593,587	**Boston**	Deval Patrick, D	1D 1R	10D
MICHIGAN The Wolverine State	Chippewa word *Michigama*, which means *great lake*	1837	58,513 9,969,727	**Lansing**	Rick Snyder, R	2D	6D 9R
MINNESOTA The North Star State	From two Sioux words that mean *sky-tinted waters*	1858	84,397 5,266,214	**St. Paul**	Mark Dayton, D	2D	4D 4R
MISSISSIPPI The Magnolia State	Ojibwe word that means *great river* or *father of waters*	1817	47,695 2,951,996	**Jackson**	Haley Barbour, R	2R	1D 3R
MISSOURI The Show-Me State	Indian word that means *town of the large canoes*	1821	69,709 5,987,580	**Jefferson City**	Jeremiah Nixon, D	1D 1R	3D 6R
MONTANA The Treasure State	From the Spanish word meaning *mountain*	1889	147,047 974,989	**Helena**	Brian Schweitzer, D	2D	1R
NEBRASKA The Cornhusker State	Oto Indian word *nebrathka*, which means *flat water*	1867	77,359 1,796,619	**Lincoln**	Dave Heineman, R	1D 1R	3R
NEVADA The Silver State	Spanish word meaning *snow-clad*	1864	110,567 2,643,085	**Carson City**	Brian Sandoval, R	1D 1R	1D 2R
NEW HAMPSHIRE The Granite State	Named for Hampshire, a county in England	1788	9,283 1,324,575	**Concord**	John Lynch, D	1D 1R	2R
NEW JERSEY The Garden State	Named for Jersey, an island in the English Channel	1787	7,790 8,707,739	**Trenton**	Christopher Christie, R	2D	7D 6R
NEW MEXICO The Land of Enchantment	Named after the country Mexico	1912	121,599 2,009,671	**Santa Fe**	Susana Martinez, R	2D	2D 1R
NEW YORK The Empire State	Honors England's Duke of York	1788	49,112 19,541,453	**Albany**	Andrew Cuomo, D	2D	21D 8R
NORTH CAROLINA The Tar Heel State; The Old North State	Honors King Charles I of England (originally Province of Carolana, or land of Charles)	1789	52,672 9,380,884	**Raleigh**	Bev Purdue, D	1D 1R	7D 6R
NORTH DAKOTA The Peace Garden State	Named for the Dakota Sioux Indians of the region	1889	70,704 646,844	**Bismarck**	Jack Dalrymple, R	1D 1R	1R
OHIO The Buckeye State	Iroquois word that means *something great*	1803	41,328 11,542,645	**Columbus**	John Kasich, R	1D 1R	5D 13R
OKLAHOMA The Sooner State	Choctaw words *okla*, meaning *people*, and *homma*, meaning *red*	1907	69,903 3,687,050	**Oklahoma City**	Mary Fallin, R	2R	1D 4R
OREGON The Beaver State	From the French word *ouragan*, meaning *hurricane*	1859	97,052 3,825,657	**Salem**	John Kitzhaber, D	2D	4D 1R

STATE NAME / NICKNAME	ORIGIN OF NAME	ENTERED UNION	LAND AREA (SQ MI) / POPULATION [1]	CAPITAL	GOVERNOR	U.S. SENATORS	U.S. REPS.
PENNSYLVANIA / The Keystone State	Honors Sir William Penn, father of the colony's founder; the name means *Penn's Woods* in Latin	1787	45,310 / 12,604,767	Harrisburg	Tom Corbett, R	1D / 1R	7D / 12R
RHODE ISLAND / The Ocean State	After the Greek island of Rhodes	1790	1,213 / 1,053,209	Providence	Lincoln Chafee, Ind[2]	2D	2D
SOUTH CAROLINA / The Palmetto State	Honors King Charles I of England *(see North Carolina)*	1788	31,117 / 4,561,242	Columbia	Nikki Haley, R	2R	1D / 5R
SOUTH DAKOTA / The Mount Rushmore State	Named for the Dakota Sioux Indians of the region	1889	77,122 / 812,383	Pierre	Dennis Daugaard, R	1D / 1R	1D
TENNESSEE / The Volunteer State	From *Tanasie*, the name of a Cherokee village	1796	42,146 / 6,296,254	Nashville	Bill Haslam, R	2R	2D / 7R
TEXAS / The Lone Star State	From an Indian word that means *friends*	1845	266,874 / 24,782,302	Austin	Rick Perry, R	2R	9D / 23R
UTAH / The Beehive State	Named for the Ute Indians of the region	1896	84,905 / 2,784,572	Salt Lake City	Gary Herbert, R	2R	1D / 2R
VERMONT / The Green Mountain State	French words *vert*, meaning *green*, and *mont*, meaning *mountain*	1791	9,615 / 621,760	Montpelier	Peter Shumlin, D	1D / 1 Ind[2]	1D
VIRGINIA / Old Dominion	Honors "the Virgin Queen," England's Elizabeth I	1788	40,598 / 7,882,590	Richmond	Robert McDonnell, R	2D	3D / 8R
WASHINGTON / The Evergreen State	Named in honor of George Washington	1889	68,126 / 6,664,195	Olympia	Chris Gregoire, D	2D	5D / 4R
WEST VIRGINIA / The Mountain State	Honors "the Virgin Queen," England's Elizabeth I	1863	24,231 / 1,819,777	Charleston	Earl Ray Tomblin, D	2D	1D / 2R
WISCONSIN / The Badger State	From an Indian word meaning *grassy place*	1848	56,145 / 5,654,774	Madison	Scott Walker, R	1D / 1R	3D / 5R
WYOMING / The Equality State	From a Delaware Indian word meaning *upon the great plain*	1890	97,818 / 544,270	Cheyenne	Matt Mead, R	2R	1R

Capital District, Territories, and Commonwealths

NAME	ORIGIN OF NAME	STATUS / DATE ACQUIRED	LAND AREA (SQ MI) / POPULATION [1]	CAPITAL	HEAD OF GOVERNMENT
WASHINGTON, DISTRICT OF COLUMBIA (D.C.)	Honors George Washington and Christopher Columbus	U.S. federal district 1800[3]	68 / 599,657	Capital of the United States	Mayor Vincent Gray, D
AMERICAN SAMOA (Oceania)	Ancient Pacific deity	U.S. territory 1900[4]	77 / 57,291	Pago Pago	Governor Togiola Tulafono, D
GUAM (Oceania)	Guahan word that means *we have*	U.S. territory 1898[5]	209 / 154,805	Hagatna	Governor Eddie Calvo, R
NORTHERN MARIANA ISLANDS (Oceania)	Honors Maria Ana of Austria, the mother of Spain's King Carlos II	Self-governing commonwealth 1947[6]	184 / 69,221	Saipan	Governor Benígno Fitial (C)[7]
PUERTO RICO (Caribbean Sea)	Spanish for *rich port*	Self-governing commonwealth 1898[8]	3,515 / 3,954,037	San Juan	Governor Luis Fortuño (NPP, R)[9]
U.S. VIRGIN ISLANDS (Caribbean Sea)	Named for the Virgins of St. Ursula, an early religious order	U.S. territory 1917[10]	132 / 108,612	Charlotte Amalie, St. Thomas	Governor John deJongh Jr., D

FOOTNOTES: [1]State, D.C., and Puerto Rico population figures: U.S. Census Bureau, July 2009 estimates; territories: 2000 Census. [2]Independents are not elected as Republicans or Democrats. Both Independents in the Senate caucus with the Democrats. [3]Date when federal government moved from Philadelphia to Washington, D.C. [4]Date a treaty with the U.K. and Germany granted U.S. control. [5]Date ceded to U.S. by Spain after the Spanish-American War; became a U.S. territory in 1950. [6]Date administration by U.S. began (in a trusteeship for the United Nations); became a self-governing commonwealth in 1978. [7]Covenant Party. [8]Date ceded to U.S. by Spain after the Spanish-American War; became a self-governing commonwealth in 1952. [9]NPP: New Progressive Party; Fortuño is also a Republican. [10]Date purchased from Denmark for $25 million.

Data compiled and edited by Mary Harvey. SOURCES: Nickname, date entered Union/acquired, capital: *The Book of the States*. Origin of name, land area: *World Book Encyclopedia*. Population: U.S. Bureau of the Census. Governors: National Governors Association. U.S. Senators and Representatives: U.S. House and Senate Web sites, news accounts. Data confirmed as of December 2010.

The U.S. in Focus, Part 2

This section offers a portrait of the nation through the use of statistics. For example, the high school graduation rates and eighth-grade proficiency levels in reading may give you an idea of how well schools are working in each state. (Note the figures for the nation as a whole in the first line.)

The table also shows how much each state spends per student on its public schools. Which states spend the most and the least? Do you think there's a relationship between what states spend and how well students perform?

Which factors here are most important to your quality of life? What would you change about your state if you could?

NAME	POPULATION		Unem-ployment rate, 2010[1]	Personal income per capita, 2009[2]	Poverty rate, 2008-2009[3]	Job growth rate, 2005-2010[4]	High school graduation rate, 2007-2008	Public-school spending per student, 2007-2008	8th graders at or above proficient reading level, 2009[5]	Violent crimes per 100,000 people, 2009[6]
	Under 18 years of age, 2009	Age 65 and older, 2009								
THE U.S.	24%	13%	9.8%	$39,626	12%	−2.8%	75%	$10,297	30%	429
ALABAMA	24%	14%	8.9%	$33,360	15%	−4.1%	69%	$9,197	23%	450
ALASKA	26%	8%	7.9%	$43,209	10%	4.0%	69%	$14,641	27%	633
ARIZONA	26%	13%	9.5%	$33,244	20%	−4.8%	71%	$7,727	27%	408
ARKANSAS	25%	14%	7.8%	$32,423	17%	−1.3%	76%	$8,677	27%	518
CALIFORNIA	26%	11%	12.4%	$42,548	15%	−6.6%	71%	$9,706	22%	472
COLORADO	24%	11%	8.4%	$41,839	12%	−1.4%	75%	$9,152	32%	338
CONNECTICUT	23%	14%	9.1%	$55,063	8%	−2.7%	82%	$14,610	43%	299
DELAWARE	23%	14%	8.3%	$39,949	11%	−3.8%	72%	$12,153	31%	637
DISTRICT OF COLUMBIA	19%	12%	9.7%	$68,013	17%	3.8%	56%	$16,353	13%	1,345
FLORIDA	22%	17%	11.9%	$38,890	14%	−8.1%	67%	$9,084	31%	613
GEORGIA	26%	10%	9.9%	$33,980	17%	−5.2%	65%	$9,718	27%	426
HAWAII	22%	15%	6.4%	$42,075	11%	−3.5%	76%	$11,800	22%	275
IDAHO	27%	12%	9.1%	$31,662	13%	−1.7%	80%	$6,951	33%	228
ILLINOIS	25%	12%	9.8%	$41,904	13%	−4.7%	80%	$10,353	32%	497
INDIANA	25%	13%	9.9%	$33,912	15%	−4.8%	74%	$8,867	32%	333
IOWA	24%	15%	6.7%	$37,623	10%	−0.8%	86%	$9,520	32%	279
KANSAS	25%	13%	6.7%	$39,263	13%	0.8%	79%	$9,883	33%	400
KENTUCKY	24%	13%	10.0%	$32,306	17%	−3.3%	74%	$8,740	34%	259
LOUISIANA	25%	12%	8.1%	$37,520	16%	−2.4%	64%	$10,006	20%	620
MAINE	21%	16%	7.4%	$36,479	12%	−3.2%	79%	$11,761	35%	120
MARYLAND	24%	12%	7.4%	$48,275	9%	−1.6%	80%	$13,235	35%	590

In some categories, numbers have been rounded to the nearest whole number.

NAME	POPULATION		Unem-ployment rate, 2010[1]	Personal income per capita, 2009[2]	Poverty rate, 2008-2009[3]	Job growth rate, 2005-2010[4]	High school graduation rate, 2007-2008	Public-school spending per student, 2007-2008	8th graders at or above proficient reading level, 2009[5]	Violent crimes per 100,000 people, 2009[6]
	Under 18 years of age, 2009	Age 65 and older, 2009								
MASSACHUSETTS	22%	14%	8.1%	$49,643	11%	−0.5%	82%	$13,667	42%	457
MICHIGAN	24%	13%	12.8%	$34,334	14%	−12.3%	76%	$10,075	31%	497
MINNESOTA	24%	13%	7.1%	$41,859	11%	−2.4%	86%	$10,048	39%	244
MISSISSIPPI	26%	13%	9.7%	$30,426	21%	−4.5%	64%	$7,890	19%	281
MISSOURI	24%	14%	9.4%	$35,938	14%	−3.0%	82%	$9,532	35%	492
MONTANA	23%	15%	7.3%	$34,794	13%	0.9%	82%	$9,786	37%	254
NEBRASKA	25%	13%	4.7%	$39,277	10%	1.5%	84%	$10,565	35%	282
NEVADA	26%	12%	14.2%	$37,691	12%	−9.9%	51%	$8,187	22%	702
NEW HAMPSHIRE	22%	14%	5.4%	$42,585	7%	−0.8%	83%	$11,951	39%	160
NEW JERSEY	23%	13%	9.2%	$50,009	9%	−4.9%	85%	$17,620	42%	312
NEW MEXICO	25%	13%	8.4%	$33,212	19%	−1.6%	67%	$9,291	21%	619
NEW YORK	23%	13%	8.3%	$46,459	15%	−0.2%	71%	$16,794	33%	385
NORTH CAROLINA	24%	13%	9.6%	$34,719	15%	−0.3%	73%	$7,798	29%	404
NORTH DAKOTA	22%	15%	3.8%	$40,727	11%	7.5%	84%	$9,324	34%	201
OHIO	24%	14%	9.9%	$35,590	14%	−7.4%	79%	$10,340	36%	332
OKLAHOMA	25%	13%	6.9%	$35,840	13%	2.4%	78%	$7,683	26%	501
OREGON	23%	14%	10.5%	$36,125	12%	−4.0%	77%	$9,565	34%	255
PENNSYLVANIA	22%	15%	8.8%	$40,161	11%	−2.0%	83%	$11,741	40%	381
RHODE ISLAND	22%	14%	11.4%	$41,324	13%	−8.0%	76%	$14,459	28%	253
SOUTH CAROLINA	24%	14%	10.7%	$32,338	14%	−2.9%	NA	$9,060	25%	671
SOUTH DAKOTA	25%	14%	4.5%	$38,208	14%	3.8%	84%	$8,535	37%	186
TENNESSEE	24%	13%	9.4%	$34,245	16%	−5.1%	75%	$7,820	28%	668
TEXAS	28%	10%	8.1%	$38,546	17%	5.9%	73%	$8,350	27%	491
UTAH	31%	9%	7.6%	$31,612	9%	3.5%	74%	$5,978	33%	213
VERMONT	20%	14%	5.7%	$39,021	9%	−3.9%	89%	$14,421	40%	131
VIRGINIA	23%	12%	6.8%	$44,129	11%	−1.1%	77%	$10,664	32%	227
WASHINGTON	24%	12%	9.1%	$42,933	11%	0.7%	72%	$9,058	36%	331
WEST VIRGINIA	21%	16%	9.3%	$32,067	15%	−0.9%	77%	$10,059	22%	297
WISCONSIN	23%	13%	7.8%	$37,398	10%	−3.8%	90%	$10,791	34%	257
WYOMING	24%	12%	6.7%	$48,178	10%	6.5%	76%	$13,856	35%	228

FOOTNOTES: [1] Members of nonfarm labor force ages 16 and up; state figures as of October 2010, national as of November 2010. [2] Income received from all sources during the year, divided by the population. (*Per capita* means *per person*.) Includes money and nonmoney income, such as benefits and government assistance. [3] Persons whose income falls below the poverty line of each state. (Poverty lines vary, depending on the size of families and other factors. In 2009, the national poverty line for a family of four was $21,954.) [4] August 2010 figures; farm payroll employment not included. [5] Representative sampling of public-school students by the National Assessment of Educational Progress, U.S. Department of Education. [6] Violent crimes are offenses of murder, rape, robbery, and aggravated assault.

Data compiled and edited by Mary Harvey. **SOURCES: Unemployed and job growth:** Bureau of Labor Statistics, U.S. Department of Labor. **Population figures:** U.S. Bureau of the Census; estimates as of July 2009. **Personal income per capita:** Bureau of Economic Analysis, U.S. Department of Commerce. **Poverty rate:** U.S. Census Bureau. **Graduation rate, public-school spending per student, and 8th graders at or above proficient reading level:** National Center for Education Statistics, U.S. Department of Education. **Violent crimes per 100,000 people:** Federal Bureau of Investigation. Data confirmed as of December 2010.

Index